The Bloomsbury Anthology of Contemporary Jewish American Poetry

The Bloomsbury Anthology of Contemporary Jewish American Poetry

Edited by Deborah Ager and M. E. Silverman

BLOOMSBURY
NEW YORK • LONDON • NEW DELHI • SYDNEY

Bloomsbury Academic
An imprint of Bloomsbury Publishing Inc

1385 Broadway	50 Bedford Square
New York	London
NY 10018	WC1B 3DP
USA	UK

www.bloomsbury.com

Bloomsbury is a registered trade mark of Bloomsbury Publishing Plc

First published 2013

© Deborah Ager, M. E. Silverman, and Contributors, 2013

All rights reserved. No part of this publication may be reproduced or transmitted in any form or by any means, electronic or mechanical, including photocopying, recording, or any information storage or retrieval system, without prior permission in writing from the publishers.

No responsibility for loss caused to any individual or organization acting on or refraining from action as a result of the material in this publication can be accepted by Bloomsbury or the author.

Library of Congress Cataloging-in-Publication Data
A catalog record for this book is available from the Library of Congress.

ISBN: HB: 978-1-4411-2557-6
       PB: 978-1-4411-8879-3
       ePub: 978-1-4411-3602-2
       ePDF: 978-1-4411-8304-0

Typeset by Fakenham Prepress Solutions, Fakenham, Norfolk NR21 8NN

We wish to thank you (תודה *Todah*) the reader

But we also have many more people to thank. Our spouses deserve our gratitude: Karen Sneddon and Bill Beverly. They have provided advice and encouragement at every step. Many thanks to David Lehman. He gave generously of his time and expertise to guide us in the right direction. We hope we used his map wisely. Thank you to all of the poets who agreed to be part of this collection and who realized just how important this collection would be to our worldwide community. Thank you to Haaris Naaqvi, our editor, who brought our proposal in front of the board for consideration. Thank you to Arielle Greenberg and Amelia Glaser. And thank you to the board and to others we may not know. We also thank the many presses who gave us access to the poems by their writers.

Contents

Invitation to the reader   xi

Abramson, Seth	1
Ager, Deborah	3
Barenblat, Rachel	7
Bass, Ellen	10
Baumel, Judith	14
Bellm, Dan	15
Bernstein, Charles	18
Biespiel, David	21
Burt, Stephen	23
Carlson, Nancy Naomi	25
Castro, Michael	27
Chertok, Alex	29
Chess, Richard	30
Cohen, Susan	34
Coleman, Elizabeth J.	37
Cooperman, Robert	40
Davis, Carol V.	43
Day, Lucille Lang	46
Desrosiers, Lori	49
Dolin, Sharon	51
Dubrow, Jehanne	53
Enszer, Julie R.	55
Finkelstein, Norman	59
Fish, Cheryl J.	62
Friedman, Jeff	64
Fuhrman, Joanna	67

Gaines-Friedler, Joy	69
Gerstler, Amy	70
Goldberg, Beckian Fritz	71
Goldstein, Ellen	73
Good, Howie	75
Gottlieb, Amy	76
Greenberg, Arielle	77
Grubin, Eve	81
Hecht, Jennifer Michael	83
Hirsch, Edward	87
Hirshfield, Jane	91
Jacobstein, Roy	93
Kaminsky, Ilya	96
Karetnick, Jen	98
Katz, Joy	101
Kerman, Judith	104
Kimmelman, Burt	107
Lader, Bruce	110
Ladin, Joy	114
Lazer, Hank	117
Lehman, David	119
Lesser, Rika	124
Levin, Lynn	126
Levine, Jeffrey	130
Levine, Julia B.	132
Loden, Rachel	137
Malis, Rachel	139
Margulius, Sandra Cohen	140
Mayer, Liat	142
Mazer, Ben	143
McKee, Colleen	145
Meitner, Erika	146

Meriam, Mary	150
Miller, Stephen Paul	152
Mirskin, Jerry	172
Moreno, Yvette Neisser	175
Neustadt, Leslie	177
November, Yehoshua	179
Novey, Idra	182
Olstein, Lisa	184
Osherow, Jacqueline	187
Parker, Alan Michael	192
Ratzabi, Hila	194
Raz, Hilda	196
Redel, Victoria	198
Rich, Susan	200
Roberts, Kim	202
Rosenberg, Liz	204
Sachs, Carly	206
Sadoff, Ira	208
Schiffman, Richard	209
Schneiderman, Jason	211
Schor, Esther	213
Schultz, Philip	215
Schwartz, Howard	219
Schwartz, Ruth L.	223
Serchuk, Peter	225
Seyburn, Patty	227
Shapiro, Alan	230
Sherbondy, Maureen A.	234
Shevin, David	235
Shinder, Jason	238
Shore, Jane	240
Siegel, Joan I.	243

Silverman, M. E.	245
Sirowitz, Hal	251
Skillman, Judith	253
Skloot, Floyd	255
Slonimsky, Lee	259
Sol, Adam	261
Solomon, Onna	263
Stein, Melissa	264
Stone, Nomi	266
Stonestreet, Lisa Gluskin	268
Sulak, Marcela	270
Taavila, Pia	272
Terman, Philip	274
Topal, Carine	280
Trousdale, Rachel	282
Warn, Emily	284
Weiner, Joshua	287
Weinfield, Henry	290
Weiser, Karen	293
Wetzsteon, Rachel	294
Zapruder, Matthew	297
Zucker, Rachel	301
Further Reflections: Commentary on Jewish American Poetry	302
Glossary	312
Permissions credits	316

Invitation to the reader

M. E. Silverman and Deborah Ager

We joined forces in 2010 in order to develop an anthology of contemporary Jewish American poetry. Did the world need such a poetry anthology? We thought so, yet we started researching to be certain. While we found a few fine examples of anthologies related to Jewish literature, the books we found did not do the following: publish writers born after 1945, focus solely on poetry, or include a wide range of American writers from all corners of the United States.

Within these pages, we invite you to consider, explore, and reflect upon what shapes the heart of Jewish American poems that both celebrate Jewish traditions and honor the human spirit. In this book, we wanted to share distinctly Jewish American voices, which include second-generation Jews, converts, those on the path to conversion, secular Jews, a rabbi, those who've made Aliyah, and others. We included poems that both do and do not focus on Jewish themes, and we did that to convey the breadth and depth of Jewish personhood. With this book, we do not attempt to answer what it means to be Jewish in a time when so many follow a secular life. We seek to answer how the long history of Judaism expresses itself in the daily lives of the artists represented within these pages, and the poems do that on their own.

Charles Bernstein, in "The Klupzy Girl," wrote: "Poetry is like a swoon, with this difference: / It brings you to your senses." We hope you, the reader, will have enough poetic sense to see beyond the categories and labels to the beauty of each word, each image, and of the ideas within these poems. We hope you take our invitation to you to read each poem, to connect to these "Jewish" American poets, these contemporary poets with multiple identities, in the hopes you gain a better understanding of the contemporary Jewish voice, in all its vast diversities and complexities, that makes each poem (whether consciously or not so apparent) part American, part Jewish, part distinct to the individual, but always beautifully human.

Shalom,
M. E. Silverman and Deborah Ager

Seth Abramson

Born in Concord, Massachusetts in 1976, he is the author of three collections of poetry: *Thievery*, winner of the 2012 Akron Poetry Prize; *Northerners*, winner of the 2010 Green Rose Prize from New Issues Poetry & Prose, and *The Suburban Ecstasies*. The Series Editor for Best American Experimental Writing. In 2008 he was awarded the J. Howard and Barbara M. J. Wood Prize by *Poetry*, and his poems have appeared in such magazines and anthologies as *Best New Poets 2008*, *Poetry*, *American Poetry Review*, *New American Writing*, *Boston Review*, *Colorado Review*, and *New York Quarterly*. A regular contributor to *Poets & Writers* magazine and *The Huffington Post*, his essays on poetry, politics, and higher education have been cited online by *The New Yorker*, *Rolling Stone*, *The Economist*, *The Los Angeles Times*, The Poetry Foundation, and elsewhere. He is a graduate of Dartmouth College, Harvard Law School, and the Iowa Writers' Workshop.
http://www.sethabramson.net

Hy-Vee

The eyes of cashiers are hard to see out of, because
earnest lies are the hardest to get out of,
and how many teams have I worn
the uniform of,
and why when we beat the others was it beating off
I was dreaming of—

and what secret was I ever the holder of,
so that when they spoke of me softly behind a door
it was really me they were speaking of,
and not the afterimage of
what I'd always hoped to be an example of,

a kind of cousin of
those young men my mother and some books
had told me of,
who could stand against whatever grief their gods
could dream of,
because something else had made the stuff
they were made of,
and there would always be a quiet life back home
they were still worthy of,
if ever they decided they had had enough of
the hard young men they'd always worn the colors of.

Poem For Battered Man

On the morning the sun is loved
by a woman
        on the right side
of the bed, a platoon of red birds
detaches from a willow
        across the river
because they aren't in love with it
and it doesn't love them back.
        For the flying
flight is easy. I have to make rent
for her
and for myself. Soon there will be
a breakup
        way up the flagpole,
the flag will flutter down to cover
its country. Not yet. Now there is
a man or woman
        dying for a stranger
on every screen, in every country.
It's what we keep
watching for, why I stay like this,
why being just one day
        in this particular sunlight
is worth the cost I'm speaking of.

Deborah Ager

She is founding editor of *32 Poems Magazine*. Many poems first appearing in the magazine have been honored in the *Best American Poetry* and *Best New Poets* anthologies and on Verse Daily and Poetry Daily. Ager is co-editor of *Old Flame: The First Ten Years of 32 Poems Magazine* and author of *Midnight Voices*. Her poems have appeared in *The Georgia Review*, *Quarterly West*, *Los Angeles Review*, and *Birmingham Poetry Review* and have been anthologized in *Best New Poets*, *From the Fishouse*, and *No Tell Motel*.
http://www.deborahager.com

Fires on Highway 192

    after Neruda's "Disasters"

In Florida, it was raining ash because the fire
demanded it. I had to point my car landward
and hope the smoke would part, but it was a grey sea
absorbing my body. Cabbage palms were annihilated.
Even the Indian River steamed. Black stalks stank.
The condominiums spit smoke into twilight.
Still, a cattle egret landed, preening, in a pasture
filled with embers – the cattle dead or removed.
And I was hungry; there was nothing to eat.
And I was thirsty and raised the river to my mouth.
And I was alone, and there was only that one egret
searching for a cow. The wind was a whisper on my tongue.
Ash on ash. Slumber shallow. I was a frown
in an unfamiliar city after sundown. Vultures circled
like assassins. I made a bed of the road. I made a pillow
of misery and slept and had no story I wanted to confess.

A Poem in Which My Father is Not the Villain

I believe we commit errors we want no one to know about,

that we wish we could bathe and be healed and sip whisky and be clean.

And when the bitter drink hits my tongue—after that first sting—

the first memory returns—

my throat swollen nearly shut with a virus,

my tonsils large as shooter marbles, swollen to touching,

attracting hospital residents who peer into my throat and take notes,

and my father cuts the whisky with water, adding ice.

If it's cold enough, you can't taste it.

Here, and he sets down the glass.

I taste it. *Drink it only if you want. It helps,* he says.

That very first sting is the one I remember now

thinking of the plate glass restaurant window at Penn Plaza,

allowed to dine with my parents after dark,

staring over my menu at the theatre where we would see a musical,

where I would sit in a red-cushioned seat and swing my legs.

The man outside the window wore a blanket. He pressed his face to the glass.

One blanket against the February night in Washington.

He knocked on the window. My father stood up and shut the blinds.

Something happened then. Perhaps it was relief. Some diners smiled.

Others looked down. I was a child and poverty had been hidden from me

even when it was my own. Before this poem turns my father into the villain,

understand he grew up with the disappeared father, the orphanage,

the lack of money. And maybe shutting that blind becomes shutting out

part of his own life, his hunger, his need. Maybe you have to shut

something out to believe the lie that everything is fine.

A Treatise on Leaving

In memory of Emilie Lellouche

I have two hearts and one is five years old and wearing a life preserver.
Last week, I slid across that river in a pontoon with my daughter and
    her class.
We looked for waterfowl and found three men who sat on blue bins.
Each held a fishing pole. My daughter smiled at them
and said they did not smile back. Not one of us refused
the life preserver. Only two of us know the names for those water birds
we see, the herons, which lived near me in Florida,
where a newspaper just reported that twenty percent of homes are
    empty.
My grandmother's house is one of those empty homes.
When I last visited her, she'd left her lipstick on a table.
She thought she'd come back. She left her checkbook out.
I did not want to touch the lipstick. I thought she'd come back.
It's Florida and the evening of a super moon. It's Florida

and a fire burns the palm trees and palmettos. Ashes float
Over the highway. It's Florida, and I am outside bent into my knees.
My grandmother's neighbor asks if I am okay.
I say I am okay, yet I'm not. I am not for lying.
I am against forgetting. The time I visited the Spy Museum
With a friend we saw how people wrapped their bodies
Around a car engine to escape a country, how others hid
in small tunnels. And I think of my friend's grandmother
Who escaped on one of the last boats from Marseille
before the Nazis stopped letting people leave.
No one knows the name for the light resting on the tip of a wave.
The passengers must have waved until those on shore became small.
In my grandmother's house, someone moved the lipstick while I showered.
While I brushed my hair, the world was changing. I could not stop it.

Rachel Barenblat

Born in San Antonio in 1975, she holds an MFA from the Bennington Writing Seminars and she is an ordained rabbi as of January 2011 by ALEPH: the Alliance for Jewish Renewal. She is author of four poetry chapbooks. Her first book-length collection of poems, *70 Faces*, contains poems arising out of each portion in the Torah. Her second book, *Waiting to Unfold* collects poems of pregnancy and the first year of motherhood. Her blog, The Velveteen Rabbi, was named one of the top 25 sites on the internet by *TIME Magazine* in 2008. She is a contributing editor at *Zeek: A Jewish Journal of Thought and Culture*. She lives in western Massachusetts with her husband and son. http://velveteenrabbi.com

Eating the Apple

The first time
I spoon applesauce

your long shiver
makes me laugh

one bite, then
you turn away

this new flavor
not yet familiar

in my imagination
I'm introducing you

to mangoes already,
to fresh bread,

halvah and tamales,
injera and kimchi

but you're not
ready for difference

or new discovery,
hot fists clinging

to the Eden
you've always known

Command (Tzav)
A perpetual fire shall be kept burning on the altar, not to go out. —Lev. 6:6

First you dress in linen
then scoop out the ashes.
Stop and wash with water,
then you change your garments

and scoop out the ashes.
Lather, rinse, repeat;
then you change your garments.
No one said it was easy.

Lather, rinse, repeat;
out here in the wilderness
no one said it was easy
to keep the fire burning.

Out here in the wilderness
there's little wood to scavenge
to keep the fire burning
all night until morning.

There's little wood to scavenge
and you want perpetual motion
all night until morning—
that's the ritual of the offering.

You want perpetual motion
but fires don't burn forever
and the ritual of the offering
is this lesson from the waters.

Fires don't burn forever
(except for that holy pillar)
so take a lesson from the waters
and the reeds you sludged across.

Remember that holy pillar
like a beacon in the darkness
and the reeds you sludged across
each shaky step toward freedom.

Like a beacon in the darkness
God's instructions on this are clear:
each shaky step toward freedom
keeps the fire burning.

God's instructions on this are clear.
Stop and wash with water.
Keep the fire burning.
First you dress in linen.

Ellen Bass

Born in Philadelphia in 1947, she has a new book of poetry, *Like A Beggar*, forthcoming from Copper Canyon Press in 2014. Her previous books include *The Human Line* in 2007, which was named a Notable Book of 2007 by the *San Francisco Chronicle*. She co-edited *No More Masks! An Anthology of Poems by Women* and has published several volumes of poetry, including *Mules of Love* which won the Lambda Literary Award. Her work has been published in many journals and magazines including *The Atlantic*, *The American Poetry Review*, *The New Republic*, *The Progressive*, and *The Kenyon Review*. Among her awards for poetry are a Pushcart Prize, the Elliston Book Award, The Pablo Neruda Prize from *Nimrod*/Hardman, the Larry Levis Prize from *Missouri Review*, and the *New Letters* Prize. Her nonfiction books include *Free Your Mind: The Book for Gay, Lesbian and Bisexual Youth and Their Allies*, *I Never Told Anyone: Writings by Women Survivors of Child Sexual Abuse* and *The Courage to Heal: A Guide for Women Survivors of Child Sexual Abuse*. She teaches in the MFA writing program at Pacific University.
http://www.ellenbass.com

Relax

Bad things are going to happen.
Your tomatoes will grow a fungus
and your cat will get run over.
Someone will leave the bag with the ice cream
melting in the car and throw
your blue cashmere sweater in the drier.
Your husband will sleep
with a girl your daughter's age, her breasts spilling

out of her blouse. Or your wife
will remember she's a lesbian
and leave you for the woman next door. The other cat—
the one you never really liked—will contract a disease
that requires you to pry open its feverish mouth
every four hours for a month.
Your parents will die.
No matter how many vitamins you take,
how much Pilates, you'll lose your keys,
your hair and your memory. If your daughter
doesn't plug her heart
into every live socket she passes,
you'll come home to find your son has emptied
your refrigerator, dragged it to the curb,
and called the used appliance store for a pick up—drug money.
There's a Buddhist story of a woman chased by a tiger.
When she comes to a cliff, she sees a sturdy vine
and climbs half way down. But there's also a tiger below.
And two mice—one white, one black—scurry out
and begin to gnaw at the vine. At this point
she notices a wild strawberry growing from a crevice.
She looks up, down, at the mice.
Then she eats the strawberry.
So here's the view, the breeze, the pulse
in your throat. Your wallet will be stolen, you'll get fat,
slip on the bathroom tiles of a foreign hotel
and crack your hip. You'll be lonely.
Oh taste how sweet and tart
the red juice is, how the tiny seeds
crunch between your teeth.

Asking Directions in Paris

Où est le boulevard Saint Michel?
You pronounce the question carefully.
And when the native stops,
shifting her narrow sack of wine and baguettes,
lifting her manicured hand,
you feel a flicker of accomplishment.
But beyond that, all clarity dissolves,
for the woman in the expensive shoes
and suit exactly the soft gray
of clouds above the cathedral does not say
to the right, to the left, straight ahead,
phrases you memorized from tapes
as you drove around your hometown
or mumbled into a pocket *Berlitz* on the plane,
but relays something wholly unintelligible,
some version of: *On the corner*
he is a shop of jewels in a fountain
when the hotel arrives on short feet.
You listen hard, nodding,
as though your pleasant disposition,
your willingness to go
wherever she tells you,
will make her next words pop up
from this ocean of sound,
somewhat the way a dog hears its name
and the coveted syllable *walk.*
If you're brave enough, or very nervous,
you may admit you don't understand.
And though evening's coming on and
her family's waiting, her husband lighting
another Gauloise, the children setting the table,
she repeats it again, another gesture
of her lovely hand, from which you glean
no more than you did the first time.
And as you thank her profusely
and set off full of groundless hope,
you think this must be how it is

with destiny: God explaining
and explaining what you must do,
and all you can make out is a few
unconnected phrases, a word or two, a wave
in what you pray is the right direction.

If You Knew

What if you knew you'd be the last
to touch someone?
If you were taking tickets, for example,
at the theater, tearing them,
giving back the ragged stubs,
you might take care to touch that palm,
brush your fingertips
along the life line's crease.

When a man pulls his wheeled suitcase
too slowly through the airport, when
the car in front of me doesn't signal,
when the clerk at the pharmacy
won't say *Thank you*, I don't remember
they're going to die.

A friend told me she'd been with her aunt.
They'd just had lunch and the waiter,
a young gay man with plum black eyes,
joked as he served the coffee, kissed
her aunt's powdered cheek when they left.
Then they walked half a block and her aunt
dropped dead on the sidewalk.

How close does the dragon's spume
have to come? How wide does the crack
in heaven have to split?
What would people look like
if we could see them as they are,
soaked in honey, stung and swollen,
reckless, pinned against time?

Judith Baumel

Born in the Bronx in 1956, she is a poet, critic, translator, and professor of English. She was Founding Director of the Creative Writing Program at Adelphi University. Her books of poetry are *The Weight of Numbers*, for which she won The Walt Whitman Award of the Academy of American Poets, *Now*, and *The Kangaroo Girl*. She is currently working on *Border Exchange: crossing into a father's mind and memory*, a hybrid book of personal narrative and literary history about the experience and memory of the Holocaust in the Polish/Ukrainian Borderlands. She blogs at: http://www.judithbaumel.com

And Boaz Begat Obed, and Obed Begat Jesse, and Jesse Begat David

So come to the planting ground, come,
come to the fields of abundance,
the sheaves that I let fall of purpose,
Come that the bright constant grasses of perennial
corn should mix its pikes and tassels,
that a husk should burst with bountiful rows.
Come to the threshing floor, come,
come that the corn which we winnow and eat
be made sweet and productive.
Come that I might spread my skirt over you,
that an August afternoon of cut grasses,
wildflowers, pines and oaks might know clouds
the white of seraphim, generous and wise.
Come to the many greens of the far hills
shifted in rippling shadow and exchange
beneath a sun coupling with those clouds,
that a full moon buffeted in a night
of quicksilver blue should stand
a sentinel of grace and fear.
And to corn that names the fruit of all
edible grasses, the inheritance we redeem,
bring your yellow, still, silent, dawn.

Dan Bellm

Born in Springfield, Illinois in 1952, he is a poet and translator living in Berkeley, California. He has published three books of poetry, most recently *Practice*, winner of a California Book Award. His work has appeared in *The American Poetry Review*, *Poetry*, *Ploughshares*, *The Threepenny Review*, *Best American Spiritual Writing*, and *Word of Mouth: An Anthology of Gay American Poetry*. He teaches literary translation at Antioch University Los Angeles and at New York University.
http://www.danbellm.com

Practice

Every seventh year you shall practice remission of debts.
Deuteronomy 15.1

How simple it ought to be, to practice compassion
on someone gone, even love him, long as he's not
right there in front of me, for I turned to address him,
as I do, and saw that no one's lived in that spot
for quite some time. O turner-away of prayer—
not much of a God, but he was never meant to be.
For the seventh time I light him a candle; an entire
evening and morning it burns; not a light to see
by, more a reminder of light, a remainder, in a glass
with a prayer on the label and a bar code from the store.
How can he go on? He can't. Then let him pass
away; he gave what light he could. What more
will I claim, what debt of grace he doesn't owe?
If I forgive him, he is free to go.

Re'eh, Deuteronomy 11.16–16.17

Psalm

redeemable, forgiven, blessed,
    by what right—only by
wanting—

    to have done
enough, to have done what is right,
    or not—

emptied out
    to make room for the unasked for,
that the soul might live—

    red poppies still bowed down
on narrowest curving stems
    after the rain has passed,

still staring
    at the darkened ground,
heedless of the light they wear—

The Weight

You must prepare to carry nothing
where you walk,

a God who cannot be seen,
a name you cannot speak—

therefore gather
the most precious of what you have,

and build me something heavy you can carry,
heavy as you want.

I will be weightless in it,

an idea, a promise,
among you, within you—

I will be unbearable. You can bear it.

Over and over you will pick it up
and set it down,

and as you wander
you will lose what you brought forth,

the ark will collapse in your hands,
the stones of the law will break.

Then you will carry me in your minds,
in your mouths—

unbearable as you want. You can bear it.

Terumah, Exodus 25.1-27.19

Charles Bernstein

Born in New York City in 1950, he is the author of 30 books of poetry and libretti, including *Girly Man*, *Shadowtime*, *With Strings*, and *Republics of Reality: 1975-1995*. He has published two books of essays and one essay/poem collection: *My Way: Speeches and Poems*, *A Poetics*, *Content's Dream: Essays 1975-1984*. He is editor of *99 Poets/1999: An International Poetics Symposium*, a special issue of *boundary 2*, *Close Listening: Poetry and the Performed Word*, *The Politics of Poetic Form: Poetry and Public Policy*, and *Live at the Ear*, an audio poetry anthology. He has been host and co-producer of LINEbreak, Close Listening, and Studio 111, three radio poetry series. With Bruce Andrews, he edited *L=A=N=G=U=A=G=E*, which has been anthologized as *The L=A=N=G=U=A=G=E Book*. He is currently Regan Professor of English, University of Pennsylvania. He attended the Bronx High School of Science and Harvard College. He is married to the painter, Susan Bee, and has two children: Emma and Felix.

Rivulets of the Dead Jew

Fill my plate with boudin noir
Boudin noir, boudin noir
Fill my plate with a hi-heh-ho
& rumble I will go

Don't dance with me
'til I cut my tie
Cut my tie, cut my tie
Don't fancy me 'til
The rivers run dry
& a heh & a hi & a ho

I've got a date with a
Bumble bee, bumble bee
I've got a date with a
wee bonnie wee
& ahurtling we will go.

Castor Oil

I went looking for my soul
In the song of a minor bird
But I could not find it there
Only the shadow of my thinking

The slow sea slaps slow water
On the ever farther shore
And myself pulled under
In the uneven humming
Of the still wavering warps

Tuneless, I wander, sundered
In lent blends of remote display
Until the bottom bottoms
In song-drenched light, cradled fold

Of Time and the Line

George Burns likes to insist that he always
takes the straight lines; the cigar in his mouth
is a way of leaving space between the
lines for a laugh. He weaves lines together
by means of a picaresque narrative;
not so Henny Youngman, whose lines are strict-
ly paratactic. My father pushed a
line of ladies' dresses—not down the street
in a pushcart but upstairs in a fact'ry
office. My mother has been more concerned

with her hemline. Chairman Mao put forward
Maoist lines, but that's been abandoned (mostly) for the East-West line of malarkey
so popular in these parts. The prestige
of the iambic line has recently
suffered decline, since it's no longer so
clear who "I" am, much less who *you* are. When
making a line, better be double sure
what you're lining in & what you're lining
out & which side of the line you're on; the
world is made up so (Adam didn't so much
name as delineate). Every poem's got
a prosodic lining, some of which will
unzip for summer wear. The lines of an
imaginary are inscribed on the
social flesh by the knifepoint of history.
Nowadays, you can often spot a work
of poetry by whether it's in lines
or no; if it's in prose, there's a good chance
it's a poem. While there is no lesson in
the line more useful than that of the picket line, the line that has caused the most adversity is the bloodline. In Russia
everyone is worried about long lines;
back in the USA, it's strictly souplines. "Take a chisel to write," but for an
actor a line's got to be cued. Or, as
they say in math, it takes two lines to make
an angle but only one lime to make
a Margarita.

David Biespiel

Born in Tulsa, Oklahoma in 1964, he grew up in Houston, in Harris County, Texas. In addition to being a regular contributor on national politics for *Politico* since 2008, he served as editor of *Poetry Northwest* from 2005 to 2010, and since 2003 he has been writing the poetry column in the *Oregonian*, making it the longest-running newspaper column about poetry in the United States. He has published four poetry volumes: He has published five poetry volumes: *Shattering Air*, *Pilgrims & Beggars*, and from the University of Washington Press, *Wild Civility*, *The Book of Men and Women*, and *Charming Gardeners*, as well as a book on creativity: *Every Writer Has a Thousand Faces*. For his writing he has been awarded a Wallace Stegner Fellowship at Stanford University, a National Endowment for the Arts Fellowship in Literature, a Lannan Residency, the Oregon Book Award, and the Pacific Northwest Booksellers Award. He is currently a member of the board of directors of the National Book Critics Circle and the president of the Attic Institute in Portland, Oregon.

Room

After it came in like a dark bird
Out of the snow, barely whistling
The notes father, mother, child,
It was hard to say what made us happiest.

Seeing the branches where it had learned
To stir the air? The air that opened
Without fear? Just the branches
And us in a room of wild things?

Like a shapeless flame, it flew
A dozen times around the room.

And, in a wink, a dozen more.
Into the wall, the window, the door.

You said the world turns to parts.
You said the parts are cunning spheres.
You said you always love the face of sin.
You said it's here, the lips and eyes and skin.

Outside the snow deepened
With heaves of discontent.
Inside, the tremor of our life
Flew in and in and in.

Stephen Burt

Born in Baltimore in 1971, he grew up in and around Washington DC; he is now professor at Harvard. His books include *Close Calls With Nonsense: reading New Poetry*; *The Forms of Youth: 20th Century Poetry and Adolescence*; *Parallel Play*; and *Why I Am Not A Toddler and Other Poems By Cooper Bennett Burt*. A new book of poems, *Belmont*, is available. He is Professor of English at Harvard. Before that he taught at Macalester College in St. Paul, Minnesota, and before that he lived in New York City, England, Connecticut, Massachusetts, Washington, DC, and Maryland.

Miami Beach

i.m. Milton Heller & Esther Burt Heller

"Perhaps the essence of being a Jew meant to live forever in a state of expectation for that which would not come." --Irving Howe, *World of Our Fathers*

To end one's life   and know it   by degrees
Like the men and women in these pictures:
In their eighties   in their seventies
One shirtless   blue jeans hooked over a paunch
With sun across his ribs   their fine white hairs

The frequent naps   the world too soon confined
To one square mile   then a square half-mile
A woman framed by full-moon glasses holds
Her tiny opal earrings in her hands
The swept-back wings   the mustard-colored steps

Front the last kosher hotel   Here fame has saved
The nautical fins and sterns   the turquoise curves

The edifices steaming in the wake
Of their expensive futures   As for these
The shirtsleeve women   men in iron chairs

The lucky   the ocean-faced   the escapees
Who squint and smile and grieve they faced the sea
The Europe it has held   with shaky hands
Who sat in the sun   on balconies younger than they
And watched their language set all afternoon

Nancy Naomi Carlson

Born in Brooklyn in 1949, she is the prize-winning author of *Kings Highway*, two chapbooks, *Complications of the Heart* and *Imperfect Seal of Lips*, as well as a book of critically acclaimed translations, *Stone Lyre: Poems of René Char*. She is an associate editor for Tupelo Press, translation editor for *Blue Lyra Review*, and teaches at the Bethesda Writer's Center. Her work has appeared or is forthcoming in *Poetry*, *The Georgia Review*, and *The Iowa Review*. She is the recipient of grants from the Maryland State Arts Commission, as well as the Arts & Humanities Council of Montgomery County.

To Melancholia, Mon Amour

Because I want to leave you
something beautiful, I will dye these sheaves of silk
blood red. You'll see them billow and rise
between pairs of stage hands— Handel's *Israel in Egypt*—

parting the sea as easy as stripping a bed.

I will make of these plagues a tapestry
thick with must and the pale infusion of moon,

or better still, a double choir—for beasts and boils,
frogs and diamonds of hail.

Let me go, and I'll rosin my bow for the whirr of flies,
or the wheels of your chariot in pursuit—
stallions black as the growing dark—

or my heart, straining like locust wings.

My Father's Hosta

I say *yes* to the square of earth he digs up
from his Rockville yard, hosta tips newly sprung.

He's afraid they'll die, left behind,
leaves lance-shaped, folded tight

like children's hands.
They come back each June,

and he takes them wherever he moves—
from his first home in Queens

to this room with a single bed.
There may not be a garden where he's headed.

"Plant them with sedge and bine,"
my father instructs, as he nudges roots.

Knowing the ground always claims
its own, I still promise to keep them alive.

Michael Castro

Born in New York City in 1945, he is co-founder of the literary organization and magazine *River Styx*. His books include *Human Rites* and *The Man Who Looked into Coltrane's Horn*, and *The Bush Years*. He has co-translated modern Hungarian poets with Gabor G. Gyukics, resulting in the anthology, *Swimming in the Ground: Contemporary Hungarian Poetry*, and a book, *A Transparent Lion: Selected Poems of Attila Jozsef*. His work has been included in several Jewish anthologies, including *Voices Within the Ark: The Modern Jewish Poets, Longshot: It's the Jews!, Sephardic-American Voices: Two Hundred Years of a Literary Legacy, Jewish American Poets: Poems, Commentary and Memoir*, and *Without a Single Answer: Poems on Contemporary Israel*.

The Transplant

I am a fugitive of the Big Apple.
Left it in my youth.
Began a quest for Truth.
Left behind the babble
of its brazen, craven towers.
Emerged into a natural space
& forged the track of hours.

I am a fugitive of the Big Apple.
Saw the garden overgrown.
Saw my actions overblown.
Saw the brambles & the briars
out on Mad Ave. blot the sun.
Whistled in the subway wind
& watched my sentence run.

I am a fugitive of the Big Apple.
Singing the Jerusalemic Blues.
Eating what I choose.
Left behind my father, split man-
hattan, shed the sea.
Snaking with the river, inward.
Planted my own tree.

Alex Chertok

Born in Bayside, New York in 1984, he is a graduate from University of Virginia's undergraduate Poetry Writing Area Program. He has poems published in *Painted Bride Quarterly*, *The Cincinnati Review*, *Potomac Review*, *Pebble Lake Review*, *Diner*, and *DMQ Review*, and has work forthcoming in *Gargoyle* and *32 Poems*. He was awarded a fellowship to the Virginia Center for the Creative Arts for the fall of 2009 and is an MFA candidate at Cornell University.

On Shoeprints

Two shoeprints in the hallway prove their own length,
or shortness, or never having been.

So, too, speaks
an eyelash on the page of an old book.

This much is certain, that the ghostlike heel
is smudged, as if a storm-flushed boy reeled in,

so to speak,
to clutch an armful of his father's love,

which is short for a bag of red apples.
So, two speak

in counterpoint, the boy whose teeth make white
valleys hissing in the heart of the fruit,

and the boy in the threshold, dreaming it.
Both are fruitless, really, toothless, in short,

ghostless fictions, hat and rubber bootless.
So, to speak

of them at all falls short. Still, loving rain,
the boy pictures orchards filling his lap.

Richard Chess

Born in Los Angeles in 1953, he spent most of his childhood and youth in Cherry Hill, New Jersey. He is the author of three books of poetry: *Third Temple, Chair in the Desert*, and *Tekiah*. He is professor of literature and language at the University of North Carolina at Asheville. He directs UNCA's Center for Jewish Studies as well as UNCA's Creative Writing Program. He has been a member of the low-residency MFA faculties at Warren Wilson College and Queens College. He served for a number of years as writer-in-residence at the Brandeis Bardin Institute in Simi Valley, California. He is now assistant director of The Jewish Arts Institute at Elat Chayyim, located at the Isabella Freedman Retreat Center. He lives in Asheville with his wife, Laurie, and son, Gabe, but also has two-step daughters, Alice and Margaret.
http://www.richardchess.com

The Bitter Herb

It can singe the sinuses
like revelation, it can squeeze
the eye like any worthy god
to draw compassion from
the deep root of the desert.
Its head misshapen as a newborn's
yanked from the birth canal,
it knows the earth more intimately
than we do.
One man, serious about the bitter
herb, wears a mask to keep
from tearing as he grinds, grinds, grinds
the horseradish and burps it
into a plastic tub to seal in its potency

for the ritual. It is as potent
as the sperm of an average teenager,
the wailing packed inside it
released only after you've chewed
the required pea-sized portion
at just the right moment of liberation.

The Jewish Angel

It doesn't answer to a Polish name
though it was once Polish, it isn't the light
going up like smoke to graze the ceiling,
it doesn't live for a cold bowl of borscht
with an island of sour cream floating on top,
it doesn't die each time it hears a sad violin.

The Jewish angel—it may be two angels,
two brothers, a farmer and a hunter,
a left arm and a right arm—this is my angel
as much as it is yours, it makes each of us
a little Jewish, each of us wander a little
from moon to moon, state to state,
it makes one of us crazy with coffee,
one of us drunk on tea.

I'm building my house out of old paperbacks,
westerns for the den, mysteries for the kitchen,
I'm saving the psalms until I've lived like David,
escaped to the woods, recruited the local birds
to my army, returned in a helmet of woven palmetto leaves
to claim my kingdom and God's, I'm polishing the candlesticks
and propping the window open, winter and spring, day and night,
for the wind.

Nothing but Pleasure

Do you know the history of light?
First God created man and woman,
and in the darkness they were one.
Their lives nothing but pleasure.
His hand moved over her form
like breath over water, her hand
moved like music through air.
But there was no music, no cello,
no flute, only the uplifted
cup of silence from which they drank.
Only when one of them, wobbly
with joy, pricked the air with speech,
only when he began to name what he felt
when he kissed her or when her palm
anchored on his belly,
only when he learned to distinguish
this pleasure from that, did the light come,
the light in which differences—in shape,
value, song—shone, the light
their children and children's children
tried to change or extinguish or ignore,
coupling with eyes closed, composing
a fugue of the amplified dark.

My People

My people drag a dead leg wherever they go.
they are like the horse pulling the cart
with a broken wheel.

My people, architects of an argument with God.
So many rooms, can't live in them all.
A room with a wall of salt,
a room stuffed with hair.

One of my people extends his hand
like a violin to a dark cloud.
Another goes with cows, grazes where they graze,
lies among them, stares with large, mute eyes
when a human figure approaches.

Someone should tell them the war is over.
Someone should steer them toward the grave sun.

Susan Cohen

She was an award-winning journalist before turning seriously to poetry, while on a Knight Fellowship at Stanford University in 1998–9. Since then, she's authored a full-length book of poems, *Throat Singing*, two poetry chapbooks, co-authored *Normal at Any Cost* which won the 2010 National Association of Science Writers award, earned an MFA from Pacific University, and has been honored with prizes from numerous literary journals. She lives in Berkeley, where she worked as contributing writer for the *Washington Post Magazine* and taught at the University Of California Graduate School of Journalism while raising two children with her husband.
http://www.susancohen-writer.com/

Viewing *Guernica* in Madrid

Their kindergarten teacher could be telling them
this imaginary horse
was not in Picasso's early drawings.
In the Spanish I cannot understand,
maybe he says once upon a market day in Guernica
the world collapsed around whole families
whose luck ran out, or did not,

from a burning building.
Maybe he mentions German pilots
high above the town, who were imagining
what would happen in that instant
when their dropped bombs stopped whistling,
while down below, a horse
was incapable of imagining

how to gallop out from under
the sky's sudden piercing rain.
When the teacher points to the wall behind him,

his class rapt, surely he explains they're lucky
to sit cross-legged before a masterpiece,
a painting people come from far away to see.
And I, who am one of those people,

look past the heads of tiny children to the painting
that takes the whole wall, and see it's not
Picasso's wailing woman trailing into ghostliness,
infant slack and cooling in her arms,
and not the bull with its bayonet horns
that makes this an object of devotion,
but the horse's gaping terror,

the horse's tongue razored sharp by pain,
the horse's leg severed and strewn,
and most of all, its dumb dying scream
still open to us decades later and so pure
in black and white—
as animal terror can be pure—
because a horse could never understand

the human imagination, no matter how long
you talked to it, how clear your diction
and enthusiastic your voice,
how careful and small your words.
I wonder if their teacher's telling them
Guernica started out in color,
but color would have added nothing.

Every Minute Drove It Wilder

Talons so meticulous they could pluck
    a kestrel from the wind, or pierce
        a vole's skull, but useless

on our deck, the young hawk flung itself
    head-first at the glass wall
        where panic trapped it, and flailed

its foot-long wings. Every minute drove it wilder.
    I watched you wrap a tee-shirt
        around your hands, step out

and sweep the bird up in its frenzy—
    holding it away from your chest
        and face and eyes—

then raise your arms to toss it hallelujah high.
    For just that beat, fully extended
        against the sky, you looked taller

than you had in years. Your hands were hawk,
    arms in a wilderness of feathers,
        an exuberance of wings.

Elizabeth J. Coleman

Born in New York City in 1947, she is the author of *Let My Ears Be Open* and *The Saint of Lost Things*, two chapbooks of poems. In 2012, she was a finalist for the University of Wisconsin Press' Brittingham and Pollak prizes. Her work has appeared in the journals *Connecticut Review, Raintown Review, 32 Poems, Per Contra, Blueline,* and *Peregrine*, among others. Her poems will appear in an anthology tentatively titled *When Lawyers Talk About Their World*, and her critical work has appeared in *Poetry Miscellany*. A 2012 recipient of an MFA in Poetry at the Vermont College of Fine Arts, Elizabeth has been the featured poetry reader at the "Periodically Speaking Series," and at Carmine Street Metrics and KGB Bar in New York City. Elizabeth is a member of the New York, Georgia, and DC Bars, and co-author of *Commercial and Consumer Warranties: Drafting, Negotiating and Litigating*. A classical guitarist as well, Elizabeth runs a consulting business and foundation whose work focuses on environmental justice.

Catskills Love

Mornings   you look old   a bit
like your father but I don't
mind just as you don't seem to mind
that as usual my life is
in disarray   the way the picture
we got in Quito of the South American
sky with the clouds that are all
the same is crooked on the wall
or that untamed look in my eye first thing
and that my hair grays as you gaze

outside   where the orange
of a monarch butterfly clashes
with a purple bearded iris
forget-me-nots on the hill remind
me of the last tufts of hair
on a balding man

So come inside   and while there's time
let's make our bodies
one like those jigsaw puzzles your
mother loved to put together
on the card table while she watched
TV in color

Prayer in Anticipation of a Guitar Recital
after Zbigniew Herbert

God of small things, big things and everything
in between, help me focus
on my beautiful six-stringed handmade guitar,
so down to earth next to a sinewy violin,
so hearty, like a peasant by a queen.

Let my ears be open, present for it all,
and let me know when to breathe, like an innocent
baby whose belly expands fully
with each breath.

Let me focus on the B minor key, like a Sherpa
fording a mountain pass
who carries a tourist's load on his back,
while he holds the nervous tourist's hand.

God of all secular Jews who lean
towards Buddhism, give me the skill and poise to play
that elegiac Bach line with fluidity,
with the ease of the Loire running through

a town in the French countryside,
a town that brews its own vintage wine.

May my Bach rendition bow
to the suffering of a parent who has lost a child,
a child who has lost a parent and to the melancholy
of Orpheus' dreams of Eurydice.

Please give me one phrase played perfectly,
just one, like a gorgeous shot, by a boy in a ghetto
somewhere—who everyone says has no chance.

Robert Cooperman

Born in Brooklyn in 1946, he is the author of 13 poetry collections, most recently *Cave Dweller* and *Troy*. He is the winner of the Colorado Book Award for Poetry in 2000, for *In the Colorado Gold Fever Mountains*. His work has appeared in *The North American Review*, *Mississippi Review*, and *The Southern Humanities Review*.
http://www.robertcoopermanpoet.com

Planting Trees in Israel: 1956

Before every Hebrew school class,
Rabbi Blitzstein shook
an official looking can:
"Trees For Israel."
Either we dropped in
all our change,
or the good rabbi sneered
we were worse "Anti-Semites
than Hitler and his gang."

What we didn't know—
despite the wall poster
of an Israeli commando
with a rifle and bayonet,
all but shouting, "Trees?
Are you kidding?"

was that all the coins
and the stray bills
we'd forgotten to hide
bought guns for Israel.

Maybe he feared
what our parents would say,

or maybe it was a winking
compact between him and them.

But how little Rabbi Blitzstein
knew about boys: for trees,
we barely begrudged him,
bared our teeth behind his back:
to be robbed of our baseball
card money. But for guns,
bullets, grenades?
We'd have rushed out
and bought them ourselves,
and not just for love of Israel.

The Jewish Kid

My old professor never tires
of hearing of the time Leo Durocher—
the great manager of the Giants—
was asked about the best pitcher
he ever saw.

Without hesitation, he replied,
"The Jewish Kid," meaning
Sandy Koufax: a leftie
with a fastball like a falcon
snatching a dove from the sky;

a curve so wicked, sluggers
cringed to barely glimpse
it screaming at their heads,
before it dropped away,
at the last, perilous instant.

For Hyman, Koufax was proof
there's life for Jews beyond
the one his mother chose for him,

had he only defied her desperation
for a college-educated, book-smart son,
though she never read anything
beyond tabloids and the racing form.

"Oh to have been Koufax!"
Hyman laments now: blind,
in poor health, but still he dreams
of an invincible fastball, a curve sharper
than the crack of a coachman's whip.

Carol V. Davis

Born in Berkeley in 1953, she twice won a Fulbright scholarship in Russia; she was the 2008 poet-in-residence at Olivet College, Michigan, and she teaches at Santa Monica College, California. She has won the 2007 T. S. Eliot Prize for *Into the Arms of Pushkin: Poems of St. Petersburg*. Her poetry has been in *Ploughshares*, *Prairie Schooner*, *Nimrod*, *Natural Bridge*, and others. She read at the Library of Congress in November 2010. Her new book, *Between Storms*, was published by Truman State University Press in 2012.

The Art of the Stitch

On the lid of a 17th century box, Queen Esther pleads with open palms
to the King. She understood a woman's power, for on the back panel
Haman swings from scaffolding,

hardly a suitable subject for needlepoint.
Other chair cushions illustrate the scandalous tale of King Solomon
and the Queen of Sheba, shown in various stages of undress.

Peering through glass on the third floor of a brownstone museum,
I am drawn to a lone tree on a box made to hold a lady's toiletries,
the tree where Charles II hid from Cromwell. I remember the family
   pilgrimage

to Shropshire to view that oak. At eight I worried there were not
   enough leaves
to hide the king, as if I could have saved him or my own relatives
whose fate my parents discussed when I was supposed to be asleep.

Now I petition for help: Teach me the art of the stitch:
French knot, ladder stitch, double cross; to learn
from the pattern maker the necessity of choice;

to master the art of the knot and tie down the pieces;
to snip and discard mistakes.

Let me unearth gold thread and silk cord,
trace the tail of a partridge, give it substance,
then set the bird free.

A Watched Pot Never Boils

How many years waiting for the pot to boil?
So many to remember: a blue enamel chipped
around its rim perched in a tiny room in Athens.
A tea kettle that stifled its whistle in Rome.
The many kitchens of my childhood.
My father was an itinerant do-gooder.
He gave up on religion but memorized
the dictum to repair the world.
As refugees poured out of Europe,
we sailed the other way on a three decked ship
out of New York harbor.
A trunk with leather straps
that tattered over the years.
I was what they called a sickly child,
feverish with coughs that shivered
through my small frame.
My mother wiped down surfaces
morning to night to kill off the microbes
waiting to leap into my lungs.
She abandoned the superstitions of her parents;
spitting over a shoulder to ward off the evil eye.
But science, she believed in, and cleanliness.
The water boiled extra long.
I caught the restlessness of my father,
bundling my own three children for a flight
that bumped its way from Los Angeles to Frankfurt,
Warsaw to St. Petersburg.

Their own lungs scarred and shredded by asthma.
We were warned of the water, parasites from the canals,
squatters in the rusted pipes.
I bought a timer and stood guard over the stove.
When the Russian government shut off the hot water
to clean the city's pipes, out came vats to boil water
for the bath, for the tub to wash our clothes.
It is now January in California.
I would like a cup of hot tea.
How easy it all is, a polished tea kettle,
the filtered water ready to boil in a minute's time.

Lucille Lang Day

Born in Oakland in 1947, she received her MA in English and MFA in creative writing at San Francisco State University; she earned her BA in biological sciences, MA in zoology, and Ph.D in science and mathematics education at the University of California at Berkeley. Most recently a staff scientist at Children's Hospital Oakland Research Institute, she previously served for six years as a science writer and administrator at Lawrence Berkeley National Laboratory, and for 17 years as the director of the Hall of Health, an interactive children's museum in Berkeley. Lucy's poetry collections and chapbooks include *Self-Portrait with Hand Microscope, Fire in the Garden, Wild One, Lucille Lang Day: Greatest Hits, 1975-2000, Infinities, The Book of Answers, God of the Jellyfish,* and *The Curvature of Blue.* Her children's book, *Chain Letter,* based on her poem "Letter from St. Jude," was published by Heyday Books in 2005. She is the founder and director of a small press, Scarlet Tanager Books. http://lucillelangday.com/

Changing Trains

We are changing trains
in the middle of the night,
those of us who knew
it was time to get off.

The country is foreign,
the unfamiliar air grows thick
with insects that glisten metallically.

We are changing trains,
our hot bodies pressed so close
I can scarcely move.

My throat is dry, a desert
spreading inside me.

Black hills in the distance
rimmed with stars, spiked
like the cells of the brain,

we are changing trains
and a strange man
hands my suitcase to the conductor,
whose face is dark and radiant.

I look back once, too late to return.
Sand covers the prints
of a desert bird.

Fingers of light from the coach
push back the darkness,
pulling me forward
toward a mapless country.
I climb on board.

God of the Jellyfish

The god of jellyfish
must be luminous, translucent bowl
the size of a big top,
drifting upside down
in an unbounded sea.

Surely this god, hung
with streamers and oral arms,
ruffled and lacy
as thousands of wedding gowns
and Victorian bodices,
created all the jellyfish of Earth.

Male and female, god created them
in god's own image:

the cross jellies and the crystal jellies,
the sea nettle and the golden lion's mane,
the sea wasp and the Portuguese man-of-war—

and gave them nerve nets instead of brains
to ensure their humility,
put statoliths like tiny pearls
in their sensory pits
to give them balance,
and placed spines on their nematocysts
so they could capture food
and would sting and burn any
living thing
that would harm them.

And the god of jellyfish
gave them ocelli
that shine like the eyes on a butterfly wing
when they turn toward the light,
and now their god watches over them
with god's own great ocellus
as they swirl and dive
in glistening cathedrals, and does not
expect worship or even praise:
the iridescence
of their umbrellas will suffice.

Lori Desrosiers

Born in New York City in 1955, her book of poems, *The Philosopher's Daughter*, was published by Salmon Poetry in 2012. Her chapbook, *Three Vanities*. Her poems have appeared in numerous journals and anthologies. She is editor and publisher of *Naugatuck River Review*, a journal of narrative poetry. Her mother, Blanche Fein, now 87, was a singer and an actress who went back to school at Sarah Lawrence and graduated in 1967. Blanche's stories were the basis for all of these poems. The poems are all from *Three Vanities*.

Grandmother's Hands

Grandmother's hands, veined, soft
petticoats she sewed floated white
on clothes line blowing far aloft
gathered on her arm for the night

petticoats she sewed floated white
by Ukraine's river long ago
gathered on her arm for the night
a man her family would not know

by Ukraine's river long ago
long brown curls, green eyes glowing
a man her family would not know
gathered her up, skirts blowing.

long brown curls, green eyes glowing,
grasped the ship's rail as wind's gust
gathered her up, skirts blowing
sad to leave, but knew she must.

children's laundry gently tossed
on clothes line blowing far aloft
gathered clothespins, none were lost
Grandmother's hands, veined, soft.

Sharon Dolin

Born in Brooklyn in 1956, she is the author of five poetry books, most recently *Whirlwind*, and *Burn and Dodge*, winner of the AWP Donald Hall Prize in Poetry. Her other books include *Realm of the Possible*, *Serious Pink*, and *Heart Work*. She has been awarded the 2013 Witter Bynner Fellowship in recognition of her poetry from the Library of Congress. Sharon Dolin lives in New York City, where she teaches at the Unterberg Poetry Center of the 92nd street Y and directs the Center for Book Arts Annual Letterpress Poetry Chapbook Competition. For 2013–2014, she is a Drisha Institute Arts Fellow. www.sharondolin.com

Your Only Music: Sonnet/Ghazal, Starting With A Line From Keats

There is nothing stable in the world; uproar's your only music.
In the middle of your life you know never to ignore your only music.

Why do you roam, restless, to Rome, or swim the sea at Lerici,
or, dreaming, ascend the Buddha terraces so Borobudur's your only
    music?

What you cannot hold, let go—or die. When the poet, estranged,
    killed herself
and child: to be or not to be the scorned of Elsinore's her only music.

You say you want to live more lives? Strive, first, to live your own.
When your flamenco heart stops, gored matador's your only music.

August, you trade car-tumult for windy thunder on the lake;
when you return to blaring asphalt, recall loon lore's your only
    music.

It takes your whole life to sing the dialect of your skin (not kin);
if you get caught in the labyrinth of ought, Minotaur's your only music.

To expiate your sins, shuckle as you pray on High Holy Days;
at the head of the year, Simah, *Baruch Atah*'s your only music.

Climbing Mount Sinai

The shock was all that ice
and my grey-bearded guide seeking
to dissuade me from
the ascent.

I scaled anyway, pointed
to my strong legs
though I slipped, could
grab no toe- or finger-
hold.

My persistence
made him
disappear.

Alone, as any Moses
would have to be,
I continued

To the summit to find a sea
beaten by winds
and a pool in the middle
into which I was supposed to dive.

Where were the tablets, I wondered.
Written on our bodies, the wind's swift reply.

Female and male
naked, side-to-side,
making a covenant
in rough water, on teeming land.

Jehanne Dubrow

Born in Vicenza, Italy in 1975, she grew up in Yugoslavia, Zaire, Poland, Belgium, Austria, and the United States. She is the daughter of American diplomats, and the author of four poetry collections, including most recently *Red Army Red* and *Stateside*. Her work has appeared in *The Southern Review*, *The Hudson Review*, *Prairie Schooner*, and *Ploughshares*. She is the Director of the Rose O'Neill Literary House and an assistant professor of creative writing at Washington College on the Eastern Shore of Maryland.

Judaic Studies
University of Nebraska-Lincoln

The department doesn't even fill a floor
but one room at the university,
fluorescents dark behind a frosted door
that answers woodenly to every knock.
No secretary waiting there to call
me *puppele*, German for little doll,
or feed me raspberry-swirled rugelach,
the sweetness now an eaten memory.
On certain days, Nebraska could be Poland,
the same blond silences of plains, each field
a golden corridor that never ends.
What happened to the open door? It's sealed,
with every light turned off, and no one home
except the wind breathing *alone, alone*.

Fasting

The tongue will recreate the taste of juice,
sipping on prayers made hot with black pepper
and swallowing a rough-edged word like *sin*—
it asks for utterance but scrapes the throat.
The world-to-come is body without pain.
But here, the body learns itself through tests:
a palm burned by a pot, an eye turned toward
the sun, a woman pressed against a man.
Heat and friction teach what food cannot,
except the food of speech, fat sentences
that sate the mouth by spilling out.
There is a space between some legs. The gut
needs emptiness in order to be filled.
A hand holds tight before it learns release.

Julie R. Enszer

Born in Detroit in 1970, she published her first book of poetry, *Handmade Love*. Her chapbook, *Sisterhood*, was published by Seven Kitchen's Press in 2010. She received her MFA from the University of Maryland and is a Ph.D candidate in the Women's Studies program at the University of Maryland. Her poetry has previously been published in *Iris: A Journal About Women*, *Room of One's Own*, *Long Shot*, and *The Web Del Sol Review*. She is a regular book reviewer for the Lambda Book Report and *Calyx*.
http://www.JulieREnszer.com

Eliyahu Ha-Navi

I imagined Elijah a middle-aged castrati
until I read and find him to be young, virile
like Ajax—the strong man of the Heebs.

I think of my own father—the strong man
of my tribe. In the basement he bench-pressed
on a small, red carpet remnant; in summer,

he'd lift weights midday in the cool cellar.
He'd emerge red-faced, glistening with sweat.
Wintertime, warmed by the furnace, he'd heft

late at night. Below, his life was fully his own—
no intrusions from daughters or wife.
Now, far away from my parents' home,

the iron men in my life lift weights,
carve pects, quads and glutes in large, airy gyms.
They cruise and shower and shave

in well-lit, public spaces. I think of my father
in our dark basement—building the body
of a gay man in stark isolation.

For him, I take comfort in Elijah.
Perhaps with his Elijahic body,
G-d will give him two tries—

the Phoenician princess Jezebel, then
an Adamic lover. Maybe after forty days
in the wilderness, after being fed by ravens

in the desert canyon, G-d will say to my father,
Elijahic one, Arise and eat,
and perhaps with strength from the second meal,

my father will walk through the desert
of public gyms, bars, quiet dinner clubs
until he reaches the mount at Horeb

where a "still, small voice" may ask,
Ma lekha po, Eliyahu? Why are you here, Elijah?
And he may answer, *I am no better than my fathers.*

But if I am asked of him,
Ma lekha po, Eliyahu?
I will translate,

Who are you, here, Elijah?
and I will reply, *You are my father.*
I could want no better.

Cruelty

Once I had a girlfriend.
We lived together,
planned to build a life—
house, kids. But as I was making
these commitments, I knew
she was not the one. I knew
we would not endure. Still
I said yes and yes and yes.

Then, fancying ourselves
pharaoh's daughter, rescuing
Moses from the bulrushes,
we adopted a dog. A midsize
black dog. We named him something.
I don't remember.... Abraham?
Maximilian? Yes, Max for short.
Neither of us had ever had
a large dog, though Max was scrawny,
he hadn't lived with a family.
He peed everywhere.
Nervous and skittish,
perhaps sensing something
was wrong. After less than a week,
we called the rescue, confessed
our failure. Our relationship ended
within days of the dog's return.

I hope Max found a good home,
a loving home; I hope
he lived a long life.
I cringe, remembering my cruelty,
especially now that my most beloved
and I have rescued a new dog.
A St. Bernard. She's adolescent
and gawky—she cannot control
her large body—sometimes she nips
at my hands, my elbows, my hips.
She eats like a horse.
I think of her as a pony,
coaxing her to eat carrots.
I love her. That head over heels
kind of love, unabashed,
beyond all reason.
Today, I fancy myself,
not pharaoh's daughter,
but Tzipporah. Mother of Moses.

She put him in the river,
then was summoned to nurse him.
I hold this orphaned dog
at my breast wishing for milk,
hoping a simple act
might atone for past sins.

Norman Finkelstein

Born in New York City in 1954, he received his BA from Binghamton University and his Ph.D from Emory University. He is a Professor of English at Xavier University in Cincinnati, Ohio, where he has lived since 1980. He is the author of eight books of poetry and five books of literary criticism, and has written extensively about modern poetry and Jewish literature. His most recent books are *Inside the Ghost Factory* and *On Mount Vision: Forms of the Sacred in Contemporary American Poetry*.

Allegory of the Song

At the disputed border the song is turned back.
Denied a visa, without proper ID,
the stateless one, begging and bluffing,
is last seen with what little it owns,
slumped on a bench outside a station
in an unidentified jurisdiction.
The stationmaster, the border guard,
the clerk at district headquarters,
claim that they dealt with no such figure
      on that particular date.

It is fifty years ago and it is yesterday
      and it is the day after tomorrow.
It is allegory because it is always allegory
and it is song because it is not quite a person,
      an agent that comes from an agency
      insistent upon what it knows.
Its arrival is always and never anticipated,
      and it is always turned back,
      has never been welcomed
in any decent country where things are as they appear.

The stories surrounding its place of origin
>   are contradictory and obscure.
The old people whisper them to their children
>   and the children to other children
and the authorities are always tolerant up to a point.
>   They all know the signs,
>   speak the same jargon:
even at distinct headquarters it is known to have been heard.

Night falls without mercy: the squads are dispatched
while the priest locks the church, thinking of his supper,
>   veal stew with paprika, roasted potatoes,
>   and the early mass tomorrow morning.
It's an easy walk, even for an old man,
but who is that hiding in the garden?

Think nothing of it: I was fighting off sleep
>   when I came upon the scene.
>   I never heard what became of it,
but it is allegory because it must be allegory,
>   and the losses were tallied long ago.
Let's climb up into the hills, away from the square
where the drivers beside their trucks blow on their hands
>   against an early frost.

Prayer

> *for Steven*

Last night I looked at the stars;
The baby in my arms.
And as I looked at the stars
Wheeling the planet round,
I knew I could not rest:
I felt as one addressed.

It brought me close to prayer
That such a thing could be.
You know, we think of prayer
As that which must be said:
What had I to say last night
To the stars' abstract light?

Cheryl J. Fish

Born in Bronx, New York, she is the author of one full-length poetry collection, *Wing Span*, and two poetry chapbooks, *My City Flies By* and *Obliging Night*. Her poetry, prose, and short fiction have appeared in *The Village Voice*, *Long News in the Short Century*, *Talisman*, *New American Writing*, *Santa Monica Review*, and *Between C&D*. Writings on Jewish spirituality and secular life can be found on the web site Busted Halo. She is the author of two nonfiction books on travel literature, *Black and White Women's Travel Narratives: Antebellum Explorations*, and *A Stranger in the Village: Two Centuries of African American Travel Writing*. She teaches writing and literature at Borough of Manhattan Community College, City University of New York, and she has been a Fulbright lecturer. Recently she was appointed adjunct professor of North American Studies in the Department of World Cultures at the University of Helsinki.

Generation X, Crown Heights (1995)

Generation X Lubavich boys
listening to Sun Ra
and getting high
eating kosher coldcuts by the pound
mingling *halakah* and vodka
can you reverse *baal t'shuvah*?
But in the streets near home, they still wear their
yarmulkes
and if momma begs, will straggle into Shul

In Crown Heights
staying out all night smoking with Rastas
on Utica—

    Six, seven, eight, ten
children in two-family homes. Studying in Yeshivas
no science, no math, no sex ed—you get married,
go to bed. Everything
is in the Talmud.
Lapsed Lubavitch boys dancing with voluptuous
Caribbean women in midnight discos
screwing maybe a secular Jew

Making Felliniesque films in Robert Dinero's academy
about their repressive upbringing
want to be the Lubavich Spike Lee
fundraising from aunts and uncles, you're their boy
Hanging out with Allen Ginsberg wanting to be seduced by
something old, also new. The Rebbe is like Elvis—has a shrine
    dedicated to him, and is sighted on the beach.
What happens to our mitzvahs if we lose our souls?
Pragmatism is not paganism, Clinton is not Reagan
Carry a beeper you will get through.

Jeff Friedman

Born in Chicago in 1950, he grew up in St. Louis. His fifth collection of poetry, *Working in Flour*, was published by Carnegie Mellon University Press in 2011 and his sixth book, *Pretenders*, in 2014. His poems, translations and mini stories have appeared in many literary magazines, including *American Poetry Review, Poetry, North American Review, 5 AM, Ontario Review, Agni Online, New England Review, Poetry International, Forward*, and *The New Republic*.

Sitting Shiva

I grew tired of the insults,
dishes cracking, phoebes
falling out of their nests,
the little misers who hoarded their coins
as if they were worth something.
I grew tired of wisdom
and those who stood on the ice
looking through the shade,
nodding their heads at misery
and those who came to bring gifts,
sympathy, plates of cold cuts, prayers,
who put our house in order,
so I would remember her as she was
or might have been. Instead, I remembered
knives whispering,
nurses in their shiny shoes,
red lines broken on digital monitors.
I remembered her swollen tongue,
cracked lips and torn sores.
I remembered a spot of sun
on black wood, earth falling.

Somebody

Somebody breaks a door
a shadow stepping out
as if to retrieve the morning paper.
Somebody smashes a bottle,
green eyes glinting in the street.
Somebody lets down her hair
and looks in the mirror
at the wrong time and lies
down in the tub, wrist opened.
Somebody reasons with his pain
as if he could strike a deal,
a working arrangement,
and the pills wait counting the minutes.
Somebody recalls the old master
pleading for death
while the young boy plunged
from the sky, his plumage in flames.
Somebody raises a knife
at God's command
and somebody sprays bullets into the bus
before it tumbles off the road.
Somebody snuffs the crow
prophesying a century of famine.
Somebody executes a parrot
for spitting out seeds.
A fire walks down the mountain.
A wave kisses the smouldering moon.
A big wind blows away another city.
Somebody tosses a bomb
in the burning bush
and nobody's talking.

Galicia

In Galicia an elephant scratches the ear of a flea,
and pigs wallow in broken clouds. In Galicia
I smear my face with the juice of celandine stalks
and climb a tree, surveying the rubble.
In Galicia water swirls and swirls.
Horsemen swing their angry torches.
Couches are filled with dung. The forest of diamonds flickers.
In Galicia I wrestle a rooster for the right to the bones.
In Galicia, three heavy white horses drink tea without me.
Rain flies sideways, feathers drifting over an empty bed.
In Galicia a crow caws over the rooftops.
In Galicia, my grandmother kisses me on the forehead,
twisting the dough for her famous knishes.
My grandfather leans closer to the Talmud, squinting his eyes.
In Galicia the piano benches are hopping while the count prays for
    rain.
and saints bathe their decapitated heads,
before robbing the tombs buried in the walls.
In Galicia I bake bread for the empress, who honors me with a ruby.
I hum to the earth where my ancestors lie. Hair grows
on the graves. Flies swarm my head.
In Galicia I ride against the Cossacks, waving my saber.
In Galicia I strike a match and fire rises to the sky.
In Galicia the pogrom starts at midnight.
Roses bloom under the moon.
The muddy river blasts white rock.
In Galicia I sleep in a coffin, and the crow
smells the flames long before they are burning.

Joanna Fuhrman

Born in Brooklyn in 1972, she is the author of four books of poetry: *Freud in Brooklyn, Ugh Ugh Ocean,* and *Moraine,* all published by Hanging Loose Press, and *Pageant* published by Alice James Books. She has long been associated with the poetry project at Saint Mark's Church, and teaches creative writing at Rutgers University and in New York City public schools.

Moraine for Bob

You were never a man
in the television sense of the word.

I was never a wild Slinky
in the sex-club sense of a toy.

You were never a tobacco store
in the Modernist sense of a trope.

I was never a snowdrop
in the candy store sense of a treat.

You were never Day-glo
in the fashionable sense of a scarf.

I was never withyouallthetime
in the username sense of self.

You were never a strumpet
in the toothache sense of an insult.

I was never a tooting horn
in the childhood sense of a game.

You were never a hole-in-my-heart
in the country singer sense of vista.

I was never a paper doll
in the pyromaniac sense of pal.

You were never a parenthesis
in the phony secret sense of a sign.

I was never red lipstick
in the pulp novel sense of a threat.

You were never a word
in the mystic sense of an obstacle.

I was never a shaking castanet
in the midnight sense of a song.

Joy Gaines-Friedler

Born in Detroit in 1954, she is the recipient of numerous awards, including The Marjorie J. Wilson Award for Excellence in Poetry, 2008, a runner-up in The Paunamouk Poetry Prize and the 2010 Allen Ginsberg Poetry Prize, and sixth place in the 2010 Writers Digest Poetry Contest. Her book, *Like Vapor*, was published by Mayapple Press, 2008. Her work is widely published in literary magazines, such as *Rattle*, *Margie*, *The New York Quarterly*, *The Pebble Lake Review*, *The Dunes Review*, *Controlled Burn*, and many others. Currently she teaches creative writing, both privately and for Springfed Arts Detroit Working Writers. She is also a Writer-in-Residence for InsideOut Literary Arts Project, teaches at Common Ground, a core provider mental health organization, and runs workshops for The Henry Ford Hospital System.
http://www.joygainesfriedler.com

How We Love Our Parents

We leave a list of disasters by the telephone
in case they call:

The sump-pump broke.
The basement completely flooded.

The garage floor is cracked.
Our circular saw was stolen.

They respond with lots of *oh-nos'*
and *oh for God's sake*.

It is how we make them happy.

Amy Gerstler

Born in San Diego in 1956, she is a writer of poetry, nonfiction, and journalism. Her book, *Dearest Creature*, was named a *New York Times Book Review* Notable Book of the Year, and was short listed for the *Los Angeles Times* Book Prize in Poetry. Her previous twelve books include *Ghost Girl*, *Medicine*, *Crown of Weeds* which won a California Book Award, *Nerve Storm*, and *Bitter Angel*.

Bitter Angel

You appear in a tinny, nickel-and-dime light. The light of turned milk and gloved insults. It could be a gray light you've bathed in; at any rate, it isn't quite white. It's possible you show up coated with a finite layer of the dust that rubs off moths' wings onto kids' grubby fingers. Or you arrive cloaked in a toothache's smoldering glow. Or you stand wrapped like a maypole in a rumpled streamers of light torn from threadbare bedsheets. Your gaze flickers like a silent film. You make me lose track. Which dim, deluded light did I last see you in? The light of extinction, most likely, where there are no more primitive tribesmen who worship clumps of human hair. No more roads that turn into snakes, or ribbons. There's no nightlife or lion's share, none of the black-and-red roulette wheels of methedrine that would-be seers like me dream of. You alone exist: eyes like locomotives. A terrible succession of images buffets you: human faces pile up in your sight, like heaps of some flunky's smudged, undone paperwork.

Beckian Fritz Goldberg

Born in Hartford, Wisconsin in 1954, she holds an MFA from Vermont College and is the author of six volumes of poetry, *Body Betrayer, In the Badlands of Desire, Never Be the Horse, Twentieth Century Children, Lie Awake Lake*, and *The Book of Accident*. *Reliquary Fever: New and Selected Poems* is her latest from New Issues Press. Her work has appeared widely in anthologies and journals including *The American Poetry Review, The Best American Poetry 1995, Field, The Gettysburg Review, Harper's, The Iowa Review, New American Poets of the 90's*, and *The Massachusetts Review*. She has been awarded the Theodore Roethke Poetry Prize, *The Gettysburg Review* Annual Poetry Award, The University of Akron Press Poetry Prize, the Field Poetry Prize, and a Pushcart Prize. She is currently Professor of English at Arizona State University.

In the Middle of Things, Begin

Bees rode the scalloped air of the garden.
The table, glazed bowls set for the afternoon meal,
trembled. A woman flashed in the archway
clutching her jewel box and an infant,
shoving them into a cart. The sleep was over.

I am near the mountain when you wake me,
the darkness ancient as the tongue
in a stone. You had slept a few hard hours
and then did not know where you were.
Small room on the Italian coast, it is strange
to us. I hear you touch things. I put up

my hand. I say *here, here*. We still
love each other. But this was years ago.
In the morning, we wander the ruins

of Pompeii, rooms cracked by golden
broom flowers, dry mosaic of a pool where
blind boy Cupid stands, the limed

jet in his loins. We step inside
the tepidarium, pale corruptions of pipe
and wall, and circle slowly the people
of ash, molded to their moment behind
museum glass. Cocooned so perfectly
in the postures of death, their bodies

tire us, even the dog's legs curled
to the tickle of stillness, torso
torgued almost playfully. We forget
it was the cloud they died from, not
the burning, not the fire. But the gray world.
Woman lying with her knees drawn up, cheek

resting on her hands. Man with his head
turned, hands flat, arms bent like a mantis
as if to push away the kiss of earth,
I am remembering them now in the middle
of things, like the married in their
separate fitful sleep. Suffocation
and climax: same slow drag of the month. Same
gouged bread of the face.

Ellen Goldstein

Born in Charlottesville, Virginia in 1975, her poems have appeared in many journals including *Able Muse*, *Mid-American Review*, *Subtropics*, *Poemeleon*, and others, as well as two anthologies, *Letters to the World* and *Rough Places Plain*.

Émigré

I left grief like a country,
driving between eager trees
lining the highway north,
my truck was packed and
the gates meshed shut behind me.
I was certain I could lose grief
just over the next hill.
And for a while I did.
But phrases came back,
familiar as a lullaby, anger
and blankness, a whole grammar
of misplaced emotion, and an accent
that takes years to fade.

The Rain Walkers

Mark us, the ones who sit at bus stops
and let the buses go by;

the ones who leave warm rooms
to walk through a thousand tiny ribs

of water, who pass each other with a nod.
Send us past banks of yellow windows,

flickering TVs, roommates laughing
under strings of lights.

Drench us with need, let life
well up from our footsteps

until the streets run with it.

Howie Good

Born in New York City in 1951, he is a journalism professor at SUNY New Paltz and the author of the full-length poetry collections *Lovesick, Heart With a Dirty Windshield*, and *Everything Reminds Me of Me*, as well as 29 print and digital poetry chapbooks. He has been nominated multiple times for the Pushcart Prize and the Best of the Net and Web anthologies. He is co-editor of the online nonfiction journal *Left Hand Waving*, and co-founder and -editor of the digital chapbook publisher White Knuckle Press. http://www.whiteknucklepress.com

One Night Stay

An old man with eyes like dead sparrows
is telling a story at the next table

in the restaurant of the Quality Inn
in Lebanon, Pennsylvania, something

about the price of scrap metal after the war.
Suddenly he lowers his voice. The Jews,

he mumbles. My wife and I look at each other.
Meat hooks. Gas chambers.

Our daughter notices. What? she asks.
I shake my head. We finish eating

and go up to our $74-a-night room
and all lie on one bed and watch TV.

The studio audience is laughing.
May tomorrow be a song without words.

Amy Gottlieb

Born in New York City in 1958, her poetry and fiction have appeared in literary journals and anthologies, including *Lilith, Puerto del Sol, Storyscape, Other Voices,* and *Zeek*. She is the recipient of a Literary Arts Fellowship and Residency from the Bronx Writers Center, two BRIO Awards from the Bronx Council on the Arts, and an Arts Fellowship from the Drisha Institute for Jewish Education. Her fiction was nominated for a G. E. Foundation Younger Writers Award and she was a finalist for the Ellen LaForge Poetry Prize. She has recently completed a novel, *The Mountain of Spices*.

Biblical Hebrew for Beginners

The *dagesh* is the dot in the center of a letter,
dwelling in the cavities of the *beged kefet*.
Know this like a lullaby, it is a madrigal in your hand,
singing you to sleep at night and mapping your route
through the black shapes that weave through your days
and take over your dreams. The *dagesh* can mean nothing,
or it can change everything—the way Rebecca looked down
from her camel to glance at Isaac, the black dots in her eyes
pulling him in, knowing permanence before she knew his name.
Something was once here, says the *dagesh*, but now gone,
dropped like a thread from a needle, a peppercorn
ground to powder, a star masked by a cloud, a stray bug
no longer a dark speck on the painted wall.
In my father's day it turned a *vais* into a *bais*,
the boys in the *cheder* bouncing their soles on the floor,
counting the minutes until their stickball game,
where they would charge from first to second,
only years before they were shipped off to war.
The empty gesture is a fiction, says the *dagesh*,
the teacups are stained; someone lived here.

Arielle Greenberg

Born in Columbus in 1972, she wrote *My Kafka Century* and *Given* and the chapbooks *Shake Her* and *Farther Down: Songs from the Allergy Trials*. Her poems have been included in the 2004 and 2005 editions of *Best American Poetry* and a number of other anthologies, including *Legitimate Dangers*, and she is the recipient of a MacDowell Colony fellowship and other awards. She is co-editor of three poetry anthologies: with Rachel Zucker, *Women Poets on Mentorship: Efforts and Affections*, which centers around personal essays by young women poets on their living female mentors, and *Starting Today: Poems from Obama's First 100 Days*; and with Lara Glenum, *Gurlesque*, based on a theory Arielle originated. She is also editing, with Becca Klaver, an anthology of contemporary poetry on girlhood aimed at teenage girls. She is editor of a college reader, *Youth Subcultures: Exploring Underground America*. She is the poetry editor for the journal *Black Clock*, a founder of the journal *Court Green*, and the founder-moderator of the poet-moms listserv.
http://www.ariellegreenberg.net/

Gospel

No stab in these hands.
No thorns. No myrrh.

No swing low.
No jubilee.

No abide with me,
not in this hymnal.

But blow me open. God.
No song in this throat,
just blow me open.

Synopsis

I will martyr myself at the stake, singing *Hear*.
A snake knew my name and caressed me.
The bush burned with ideas.
I was speechless; I was a ruby.
Every generation fashions an enemy.
I hid under a trapdoor in Spain, crying half-language.
Coveting, coveting, yes, no, like a jezebel on a rooftop terrace.
I eat nothing containing cartilage.
The oven is full of rock salt.
I went with my brother to interpret his stammering.
The first-born son must fast all morning.
I entered a beauty contest of strangers.
The rains lasted forever, like white dresses.
A dove came by with a postcard.
I killed my brother and hid.
There were dreams of stars and wheat.
The graves are decorated with only stones.
I took a literal train to my death. It was on time.
Boys are plied with wine and snipped.
I pray according to daylight.
Next year will return to the city of gold.
I shield my eyes from the priests' blessing.
Girls get two candles each.
I stood at the bottom of a mountain with my soul.
A very small parcel of real estate was promised.
I was taken for a fool by my village to make a story.
He offered the angels his most finely sifted flour.
I hid in an attic with my diary.
The tents are goodly.
I was a lost tribe and came out black.
Each breastplate held a dozen precious gems.
The sea boiled and horses drowned.
I hope not to be inscribed in the book of the damned.
A drop of oil burned for eight days.
I win money made of bitter chocolate.

The cat swallows the chicken, and the reaper swift behind.
I made love to my king like a sibling in a cave.
Three, four, eight, eighteen, forty, one hundred and twenty.
Trees are planted like children there.
I pretended to be my younger sister under the veil.
Manna rained down and tasted like muffins.
I looked back and was turned to salt.
Rams, bulls, lambs and billy goats.
I offered you something clean from a well.
A prophet slips in the door to drink from his cup.
I hid from God and was found.

Exodus 1:6-11

A king went down like the sun behind a hill,
slipping in his golden throne, and a king arose
and the third time a charm: that king
did not know my name.
Did not know our names, how they end
in mountains of stone.

We mean to say he did not know any promise ever made,
or the dream of wheat, or of stars.
A hundred years could have passed
between the first book and these next four
for all he did not know of us.
he was unlike any relations, this new king.

And here we live in the dead city,
winding our favored corpses in dry cloth,
wanting what wants us back
and so do not eat with other wanting.

We reckon with sand. We build the pyramids.
There's a story that goes
in every generation there will be only eleven
who are any good. Another goes

in every generation there will be one who may destroy you.
We suppose the rest stand in corners.

We are getting good at corners.
We miter bricks and have this dull hymn
as our grace:
God are the things we do not control.

Eve Grubin

Born in New York City in 1970, her book of poems, *Morning Prayer*, appeared in 2006 from Sheep Meadow Press. Her poems have appeared or are forthcoming in many literary journals and magazines, including *The American Poetry Review*, *The Virginia Quarterly Review*, *The New Republic*, and *Conjunctions*, where her chapbook-size group of poems was featured and introduced by Fanny Howe. Her essays have appeared in various magazines and anthologies, including *The Veil: Women Writers on Its History, Lore and Politics*. Jean Valentine: *This-World Company*. Eve was the programs director at the Poetry Society of America for five years. She taught poetry at The New School University for seven years and taught in the graduate creative writing program at the City College of New York. She is a lecturer at New York University in London where she teaches Creative Writing and runs the Literary Club. She is a tutor at the Poetry School, and she is the Poet in Residence at the London School of Jewish Studies. She studied at the Drisha Institute for Jewish Education and Medreshet Rachel V'Chaya College of Jewish Studies.

The Buried Rib Cage

Eve slipped from its arced ridge—
the only body part
you don't
        do evil with:

the eye, the hand,
might beg
        corruption;

the ribs are modest
shy crests, ticklish,

an open fan,
not quite sexual, yet not puritan:

delicate accordion
       —yawn, moan—
Soul breathes through its comb.

The Nineteenth-Century Novel

Sometimes I just want to give in, become
the heroine in a great nineteenth-century novel,
an earnest and suffering young woman
who makes the decision that will ruin
the rest of her life.

Once the decision has been made
I want—in my white nightgown—
to unlatch the shutter, throw
open the window,
cry out into the rain.

If not Cathy could I at least be
Elizabeth Bennet living
on the precipice of vast disappointment,
on the edge of loneliness and family shame.
To dip just under the surface of the worst
and then be pulled out
just in time.

Jennifer Michael Hecht

Born in Glen Cove, New York in 1965, Hecht is the author of the bestseller *Doubt: A History*, which demonstrates history of religious and philosophical doubt all over the world, throughout history. Her other books include *The End of the Soul: Scientific Modernity, Atheism, and Anthropology* won the Phi Beta Kappa Society's 2004 Ralph Waldo Emerson Award, and, *The Happiness Myth*, which brings a skeptical eye to modern wisdom about the good life, has been translated into several languages. Her latest work of prose is *Stay: A History of Suicide and the Philosophies Against It*, which is a moral argument in favor of living. Her newest poetry book is *Who Said*; her others are *Funny* and *The Next Ancient World*, which won the Poetry Society of America's Best First Book Award. Hecht's prose and poetry appear in *The New York Times*, *The New Yorker*, *The Boston Globe*, and *The Washington Post*. She earned her Ph.D in the History of Science from Columbia University in 1995 and now teaches in the MFA program of The Graduate Writing Program of The New School University. http://www.jennifermichaelhecht.com

Three Boats, One Afternoon

It's a flood and the water is up to the first floor
windows and most of the many are gone already.

At his second-floor desk, the man protests calmly
that life will save him. Now he's on the roof

watching the water edge up the eaves and a boat
goes by. Inside, mottled people hail him in.

He demurs, *Life will save me*. Then another
boat, and another, and all the time more water.

Finally, the tide overtakes his feet and his heart
and his nose. Dead now, and angry, the man

screams out at life, *How could you thus
betray me?* Life shows up, like God

in the book of Job; says, *I sent three boats.*

II

How many boats? It seemed like a fleet.
Years ago, when we'd likely die by thirty-five,

the first boat in the harbor must have been
an ideal ride, but now, for instance,

no one ever dies. There is always something
wrong with the equation, since, by turns, every
body dies. Also, there is the possibility of swimming.

III

At his second floor desk, the man protests calmly;
then he's on the roof, watching the water.

All right, fine, I'll get in your boat, says the man
this time, tamed by his last demise. Now he's wet

and shivering, bailing rain cups out of the keel.
His house, by now, is gone, no way to go back

to its sloping roof and drown on it now. He
imagines its thick backyard brambles,

its hyacinth, its capacity to soak up days
of rain. From this ludicrous predicament,

the boat being drowned from above, the bailing
man lets out a moan regarding the quality

of his choices. What can we now admit?
Commitment to a course of action,

or perhaps two. Three boats? One afternoon.
Now he wonders whether he picked the right
boat and where they're going. Where will
he live? The simple fact of having saved himself

blurred by the ongoing peril. Mottled
people in the other boats nod him in bypassing.

Somewhere in the expanse of water behind him
is the square half-acre that once was home.

At last, in the boat, rising rainwater overtakes
his feet and knees and nose. Once again,

as in the other version, down he goes.
The argument for one choice over

the other turns out to be the value of a daydream
dreamt in the course of his day-long lifeboat

ride. The dream was of himself bounding upon
the exploding and yet foreboding clouds,

soothing them with his easy stride until they
were fair and pale again, and turned to air.

Naked

The reason you so often in literature have a naked woman
walk out of her house that way, usually older, in her front garden
or on the sidewalk, oblivious, is because of exactly how I feel right now.

You tend to hear about how it felt to come upon such a mythical
   beast,
the naked woman on the street, the naked man in a tree, and that
   makes
sense because it is wonderful to take the naked woman by the hand

and know that you will remember that moment for the rest of your life

because of what it means, the desperation, the cataclysm of what it takes
to leave your house naked or to take off your clothes in the tree.

It feels good to get the naked man to come down from there by a series
of gentle commands and take him by the elbow or her by the hand and lead
him to his home like you would care for a bird or a human heart.

Still if you want instead, for once, to hear about how the person came to be
standing there, naked, outside, you should talk to me right now, quickly,
before I forget the details of this way that I feel. I feel like walking out.

Edward Hirsch

Born in Chicago in 1950, he is currently the president of the John Simon Guggenheim Memorial Foundation, and in 2008 he was elected a Chancellor of the Academy of American Poets. His first collection of poems, *For the Sleepwalkers*, was published in 1981 and went on to receive the Lavan Younger Poets Award from the Academy of American Poets and the Delmore Schwartz Memorial Award from New York University. His second collection, *Wild Gratitude*, received the National Book Critics Circle Award. Since then, he has published several books of poems, most recently *Special Orders*, *Lay Back the Darkness*, *On Love*, *Earthly Measures*, and *The Night Parade*. He is also the author of the prose volumes *The Demon and the Angel: Searching for the Source of Artistic Inspiration*, *Responsive Reading*, and the national bestseller *How to Read a Poem and Fall in Love with Poetry*. Most recently, he published *Poet's Choice*, which collects three years worth of his weekly essay-letters running in the *Washington Post Book World* and *The Living Fire*: New and Selected. He has been a professor of English at Wayne State University and the University of Houston.

Yahrzeit Candle

You've lit a candle on the counter between us,
a twenty-four hour mantra to your mother's passing
from one realm to another twenty years ago,

distillation of grief, wick of suffering,
rememberance of how, after the stark drama
of her last illness, the tragic final act,

we ushered her out of her suburban home
like a pilgrim and handed her over to darkness,
releasing her spirit to the air, a wing,

and turning back to each other in light
of our fresh role as keepers of the dead,
initiates of sorrow, inheritor of prayers,

Lord, which we recite but cannot believe,
grown children swaying to archaic music
and cupping the losses, our bowl of flame.

For the Sleepwalkers

Tonight I want to say something wonderful
for the sleepwalkers who have so much faith
in their legs, so much faith in the invisible

arrow carved into the carpet, the worn path
that leads to the stairs instead of the window,
the gaping doorway instead of the seamless mirror.

I love the way that sleepwalkers are willing
to step out of their bodies into the night,
to raise their arms and welcome the darkness,

palming the blank spaces, touching everything.
Always they return home safely, like blind men
who know it is morning by feeling shadows.

And always they wake up as themselves again.
That's why I want to say something astonishing
like: Our hearts are leaving our bodies.

Our hearts are thirsty black handkerchiefs
flying through the trees at night, soaking up
the darkest beams of moonlight, the music

of owls, the motion of wind-torn branches.
And now our hearts are thick black fists
flying back to the glove of our chests.

We have to learn to trust our hearts like that.
We have to learn the desperate faith of sleep-
walkers who rise out of their calm beds

and walk through the skin of another life.
We have to drink the stupefying cup of darkness
and wake up to ourselves, nourished and surprised.

Elegy for the Jewish Villages
after Antoni Slonimsky

The Jewish villages in Poland are gone now—
Hrubieszrow, Karczew, Brody, Falenica …
There are no Sabbath candles lit in the windows,
no chanting comes from the wooden synagogues.

The Jewish villages in Poland have vanished
and so I walked through a graveyard without graves.
It must have been hard work to clean up after the war:
someone must have sprinkled sand over the blood,
swept away footprints, and whitewashed the walls
with bluish lime. Someone must have fumigated
the streets, the way you do after a plague.

One moon glitters here—cold, pale, alien.
I stood in the dark countryside in summer, but
I could never find the two golden moons of Chagall
glittering outside the town when the night lights up.
Those moons are orbiting another planet now.

Gone are the towns where the shoemaker was a poet,
the watchmaker a philosopher, the barber a troubadour.

Gone are the villages where the wind joined Biblical songs
with Polish tunes, where old Jews stood in the shade
of cherry trees and longed for the holy walls of Jerusalem.

Gone now are the hamlets that passed away
like a shadow that falls between our words.

I am bringing you home the story of a world—
Hrubieszrow, Karczew, Brody, Falenica ...
Come close and listen to this song—
the Jewish villages in Poland are gone now—
from another one of the saddest nations on earth.

Jane Hirshfield

Born in New York City in 1953, she graduated from Princeton University in 1973, with the first class to include women. She is the author of seven books of poetry, most recently *Come, Thief*. Her 2001 collection, *Given Sugar, Given Salt*, was a finalist for the National Book Critics Circle Award in poetry, and her 2006 collection, *After*, was named a best book of the year by *The Washington Post*, *San Francisco Chronicle*, and England's *Financial Times*. She is also the author of a now-classic collection of essays, *Nine Gates: Entering the Mind of Poetry*, and the editor of four books collecting and co-translating the work of poets of the past, including *Women in Praise of the Sacred: 43 Centuries of Spiritual Poetry by Women*, *The Ink Dark Moon: Poems by Komachi and Shikibu, Women of the Ancient Japanese Court*, and a recent best-selling Kindle Single, *The Heart of Haiku*. Her work has appeared in *The New Yorker*, *The Atlantic*, *The Washington Post*, *The Times Literary Supplement*, *Poetry*, *The American Poetry Review*, *Orion*, and seven editions of *The Best American Poetry*. Though never a full time academic, she has taught in Bennington College's low-residency MFA Writing Seminars and at University of California, Berkeley, Duke University, the University of Cincinnati, the University of Virginia, and elsewhere, and has read and lectured at festivals and universities in China, Japan, Poland, Lithuania, England, Ireland, Canada, and throughout the United States. She has received fellowships from the Guggenheim and Rockefeller foundations, the National Endowment for the Arts, and the Academy of American Poets, and in 2012 was elected a Chancellor of the Academy of American Poets. She lives in the San Francisco Bay Area.

In A Kitchen Where Mushrooms Were Washed

In a kitchen where mushrooms were washed,
the mushroom scent lingers.

As the sea must keep for a long time the scent of the whale.

As a person who's once loved completely,
a country once conquered,
does not release that stunned knowledge.

They must want to be found, those strange-shaped, rising morels,
clownish puffballs.

Lichens have served as a lamp-wick.
Clean-burning coconuts, olives.
Dried salmon, sheep fat, a carcass of petrel set blazing:
light that is fume and abradement.

Unburnable mushrooms are other.
They darken the air they come into.

Theirs the scent of having been traveled, been taken.

Roy Jacobstein

Born in Detroit in 1948, he is the author of five collections of poetry, including *Fuchsia in Cambodia*, *A Form of Optimism*, and *Ripe*. His poetry has received the James Wright Poetry Prize, Special Mention in the Pushcart Prize anthology, and the American Anthropology Association's Humanistic Poetry Award; it has also been featured in Ted Kooser's American Life in Poetry, included in Mc-Graw-Hill's textbook *LITERATURE: Reading Fiction, Poetry & Drama*, and read on the BBC. He is a former official of the U.S. Agency for International Development and works for a New York-based nonprofit organization to advance women's reproductive health in Africa and Asia. He lives in Chapel Hill, where he is an Adjunct Professor of Maternal and Child Health at the University of North Carolina School of Public Health.

Safari, Rift Valley

Minutes ago those quick cleft hoofs
lifted the dik-dik's speckled frame.
Now the cheetah dips her delicate head
to the still-pulsating guts. Our Rover's
so close we need no zoom to fix the green
shot of her eyes, the matted red mess
of her face. You come here, recall a father
hale in his ordinary life, not his last bed,
not the long tasteless slide of tapioca.
This is the Great Rift, where it all began,
here where the warthogs and hartebeest
feed in the scrub, giraffes splay to drink,
and our rank diesel exhaust darkens the air
for only a few moments before vanishing.

Autumn Geometric

Must be another whitewashed wafer's
slithered through the slot of the celestial
jukebox: a drachma or piastre or shekel,
coin of the realm in some sere yet ever-
inhabited ancient land. Enter the theme,
borne on strings--bouzouki or oud,
dark fingers schooled in the eternal
minor key of rain, dust and olive tree.
Heat rises, worlds turn, leaves shudder
in wind, apples fall in the fullness of fall.
And in all this Earth's thousand lacerated,
lacerating tongues--in field, souk,
or shopping mall--skin of the fruit
yields to the teeth and flesh concedes
the juices that slide down your throat.

La Création

    Chagall Museum, Nice

Naked, from out the blue vortex,
a grown man lightly borne
in a blue-winged angel's arms
bends his head to the staggering light,
a man newly born, looking
to the world above, the world
of fish and the yellow moon
and the woman curved like a giant red ear,
the red sun, swirling, blown
out of an angel's horn,
the ram-headed man with the red Torah,
the *shtetl*, the rabbi, the ladder,
the menorah's nine lemony flames,
the purple-breasted women,
the blue lyre held by the blue king,

the donkey, lion, goat,
the golden fish with hands for fins,
the bearded butterfly. Above,
above His Son swaying on the white Cross,
flaccid abdomen covered at the groin
by a gray-fringed prayer shawl,
above it all, disembodied, two hands,
the visible hands of hiding
God, proffer twin tablets shaped
like pale loaves, or gravestones,
and I put my arm around my new wife's waist,
and she puts her arm around mine,
and we hold like that a minute
in that white room, in that white light,
infinite wavelets of white light.

Ilya Kaminsky

Born in Odessa in 1977, he came to the US in 1993 and was given asylum. He is the author of *Dancing in Odessa*, named Best Poetry Book of 2004 by *Foreword Magazine*. His anthology of 20th-century poetry in translation, *Ecco Anthology of International Poetry*, was published by HarperCollins in 2010. Currently, he teaches at San Diego State University.

Author's Prayer

If I speak for the dead, I must leave
this animal of my body,

I must write the same poem over and over,
for an empty page is the white flag of their surrender.

If I speak for them, I must walk on the edge
of myself, I must live as a blind man

who runs through rooms without
touching the furniture.

Yes, I live. I can cross the streets asking "What year is it?"
I can dance in my sleep and laugh

in front of the mirror.
Even sleep is a prayer, Lord,

I will praise your madness, and
in a language not mine, speak

of music that wakes us, music
in which we move. For whatever I say

is a kind of petition, and the darkest
days must I praise.

Dancing in Odessa

We lived north of the future, days opened
letters with a child's signature, a raspberry, a page of sky.

My grandmother threw tomatoes
from her balcony, she pulled imagination like a blanket
over my head. I painted
my mother's face. She understood
loneliness, hid the dead in the earth like partisans.

The night undressed us (I counted
its pulse) my mother danced, she filled the past
with peaches, casseroles. At this, my doctor laughed, his granddaughter
touched my eyelid—I kissed

the back of her knee. The city trembled,
a ghost-ship setting sail.
And my classmate invented twenty names for Jew.
He was an angel, he had no name,
we wrestled, yes. My grandfathers fought

the German tanks on tractors, I kept a suitcase full
of Brodsky's poems. The city trembled,
a ghost-ship setting sail.
At night, I woke to whisper: yes, we lived.
We lived, yes, don't say it was a dream.

At the local factory, my father
took a handful of snow, put it in my mouth.
The sun began a routine narration,
whitening their bodies: mother, father dancing, moving
as the darkness spoke behind them.
It was April. The sun washed the balconies, April.

I retell the story the light etches
into my hand: *Little book, go to the city without me.*

Jen Karetnick

Born in Livingston, New Jersey in 1968, she now resides in Miami on the last acre of a historical orchard with her husband, a nice Jewish doctor; two children; three dogs, three cats; and 14 mango trees. She is the author/co-author of nine books, including three collections of poetry: *Necessary Salt*, and *Bud Break at Mango House*, which won the Portlandia Press Chapbook Award, and *Landscaping for Wildlife*. Her poetry, drama, fiction, essays and lifestyle journalism have been widely published in magazines and journals, including *Carpe Articulum*, *Cimarron Review*, *Forbes.com*, *The Miami Herald*, *The New York Times*, *North American Review*, *The Greensboro Review*, *River Styx*, and *Southern Living*. A restaurant critic for *Miami Magazine* as well as the Creative Writing Director for Miami Arts Charter School, she also writes cookbooks, including *Mango*.
http://www.jenkaretnick.com

Asparagus Announcing Fall
--from a dish by Chef Nir Zook

Choose your steps like hand grenades.
In Tel Aviv, it is not construction
but archaeological excavation
that requires the knowledge of barricades,

makeshift though they might be,
with plywood and plastic chicken wire
sprouting unexpectedly anywhere:
the cafe where you took your coffee,

the backyard where you wanted to plant
a pool, the sidewalk in front of your office.
Between Jaffa Bar and Cordelia, the space
being renovated for more tables now can't

be fully scaled thanks to such discoveries,
though it's difficult to see the value in such depths
despite the pots of wax burning like faith.
Outside this city built on so many other cities,

asparagus is coaxed to grow from desert crowns,
takes years to establish its perennial foot.
If you fill the bed too quickly, the roots
will suffocate, but do allow the ferns to brown,

feeding the spears that someday will poke
through the crisp, golden ground. Expect beetles, rust.
Forbid yourself a knife. Elsewhere, asparagus
heralds spring, but at this restaurant, for your sake,

seared tines of khaki green stretch and splay
like a forgotten rake over a bed of crushed
yellow lentils, so many leaves pushed
into a pile where only visitors might think to play.

Doreen Kerner Dance Studio

In the days of *Saturday Night Fever*
and doing the hustle during a season of bar-mitzvahs
that lined up like hurricanes, it was junior high school
de rigeur to take Tuesday evening dance lessons
with Doreen Kerner and her daughter Andy, who modeled
jazz pants that were precursors to flowing yoga wear
and Capezios that all the kids coveted (and that the Kerners
conveniently sold in an adjoining store), forty twelve-year-olds
dying to kick-ball-change with that same heart-breaking snick
of heel. Instead most of us ran up static electricity in our socks,
the boys doing their best John Travolta impressions, arms
splayed umbrellas, invitations for lightning, the girls applying
their own conduits for bolts from the blue in the form of fresh
Bonne Belle blueberry lip gloss that the bolder of the bunch
had palmed from the pharmacy. All four walls were mirrored,

even the back of the door, which once closed turned the room
into some sort of terrible funhouse that allowed no escape
from your bad-ass or just plain bad self. Status was obvious:
those with the right gear, the most professionally smooth bi-levels,
learned the latest line dances in front. Those were the names
Doreen Kerner recited out loud at the end of each class
as if they were best-in-show purebreds, citing effort—not talent,
of course—and progress: Angela Smith. Christina St. John.
Diana Johnson. I wanted nothing more than to be
a name. Before each lesson I ate spinach, a new technology
from Seabrook Farms, creamed and frozen in a bag that you boiled
in water and then squeezed onto your plate like a tube of oil paint,
once it was cool enough to keep your fingers from being scalded scarlet,
though whether it was for strength or comfort I couldn't quite tell you.
Despite Doreen Kerner I loved this dish so much I later requested
creamed spinach at my own bat-mitzvah party, where it was poured
into a jaggedly halved tomato, leaking magenta juice, and where
I was the only newly christened adult to down it, despite the danger,
ever-present, of gooey greens getting caught in the maze of bands
and wires that had just been wedded to my teeth. Still, I spent
each session mechanical as a clock, hand-clapping until Andy
swept in for Donna Summer's "Last Dance," and chose a student
to demonstrate advanced moves while Doreen Kerner made her picks.
It wasn't until the last class when "The Time Warp" 45 hit
the turntable that I knew what I had been waiting for. "It's just a jump
to the left," and I did, leaping far to the side, straight into a virtual
Rocky Horror Picture Show where I could throw cold toast and rice,
shoot water guns at a movie screen while wearing nothing
more than frizzy hair and a corset, and interrupt the tired dialogue,
night after night. Doreen Kerner called my name then, last, almost
like an afterthought. But it was too late. It took only one "Dammit,
Janet," for me to find my place.

Joy Katz

Born in Newark, New Jersey, at Beth Israel Hospital in 1963, she is the author of three poetry collections: *All You Do is Perceive*, a National Poetry Series finalist, *The Garden Room*, and *Fabulae*. Trained in industrial design, she worked as a graphic designer before starting to write poetry. Honors for her work include fellowships from the NEA and Stanford's Wallace Stegner program. Her poems are collected in three volumes of *The Best American Poetry*; her poems and prose appear in *American Poetry Review*, *Notre Dame Review*, *Ploughshares*, *The New York Times Book Review*, and elsewhere. She currently teaches in the graduate writing program at Chatham University and lives in Pittsburgh with her husband and young son.
www.joykatz.com

Following the Orthodox Men

through the diamond district, their black-suited, shoulder-to-
    shoulder lines
moving like script through the packed streets, past rubies and corals
polished as a girls' knees, into bare metallic offices where they,
the Orthodox men, in their morning coats and white shirts
are the buyers and the sellers of diamonds
and diamonds only, offerings of the earth as odorless as prayer,
diamonds sifting into the creases of white paper, coarse and
    crystalline as the salt
that drains the blood from meat and purifies—and if I could belong
to the Orthodox men, if my body were modesty draped with linen,
my eyes cast down and my neck curved as the nail clippings

my grandfather wrapped and blessed and tossed into the stove
on Fridays—cuttings of the body made sacred—but I didn't choose
to be cut off from them and their God forever, or maybe
I did, from the moment I, as a girl, drew God—
who is never permitted to be drawn—with wild hair the color of
   sapphire.

In the Old Jewish Cemetery, Prague

The dead here, impacted in their ascent
like molars in a small jaw,
                    and the living
who skit about in the bone light
     of trying to say something to them
and to each other—
               effaced of name, broken, jammed-in,
the headstones after all say nothing:
     they bite into the footpath,
         a bad perforation between worlds.

    We leave pebbles
on this heave of graves, leave stones that are like boils
     or the heads of tacks
or bells to charm the natives
               stay down, stay down

I think the dead are not more holy.
                  How do we know they
         in their inverted world trail stars for us?
I would say something irreverent about someone
buried here, if I knew her—
              I think the dead say nothing
anyway; it is too noisy with this din
of gray alphabet, this empty trail of thought balloon
and my own radioactive stone—
               a falsehood, an

embarrassment, dot of a question mark,
                               something inarticulate
like a baby who cries out at night
             just to see if its own voice is there

Judith Kerman

Born in Bayside, New York in 1945, she has published eight books or chapbooks of poetry, most recently *Galvanic Response*, the bilingual collection, *Plane Surfaces/Plano de Incidencia*, with Spanish translations by Johnny Durán, and two books of translations of poetry, *Praises & Offenses: Three Women Poets from the Dominican Republic* and *A Woman in Her Garden: Selected Poems of Dulce María Loynaz*. She runs Mayapple Press and was founding editor of *Earth's Daughters*. She is the founder/coordinator of the Rustbelt Roethke Professional Writers' Retreat and has led community writing groups since 1991. She relocated from Michigan to Woodstock, New York in summer 2011.

http://judithkerman.com

Vessels

Carrying a bowl of hot
soup across a wet tile floor
Climbing a ladder with a storm window
Dancing with someone new
Thinking of a dying friend

The Midrash says
there was an earlier creation

It did not hold

Perhaps there was too much
holiness
the harsh law, adamant
could not hold
the particles rushed
in every direction

Sitting alone in the dark
listen

Is the holy
everywhere?
How shall I see it?

The Midrash says
holy was everywhere
filling space and time

To make room for us
it withdrew
to make room for us.

Imagining Sukkot
    Your tents, O Yaacov

The children camped
across the desert 40 years
with never any rain to fall on them
holes in a roof
not solid anyway but thatched
with branches

the delusion that there could be
stone palaces
now the kids want to
put up a nylon tent
next to the barbecue
they giggle at crackling branches
the possum who lives
under the neighbor's shed
scuffles through the leaves
and stares eyes glowing red
into the flashlight
starlight gleams through gaps
in the dark branches as suburbanites
try to sleep on an air mattress
on a pressure-treated deck

in the backyard of a house
the silence never absolute
the sound of freeway traffic
carried miles on the wind

once a year for a week
hoping it won't rain.

Burt Kimmelman

Born in Brooklyn in 1947, he has published eight collections of poetry – *Gradually the World: New and Selected Poems, 1982–2013, The Way We Live, As If Free, There Are Words, Somehow, The Pond at Cape May Point*, a collaboration with the painter Fred Caruso, *First Life*, and *Musaics*. He has also published a number of books of literary criticism, including *The "Winter Mind": William Bronk and American Letters*, and scores of essays on medieval, modern, or contemporary poetry. Recent interviews of Kimmelman are available online: with Tom Fink in *Jacket* 40 (text), and with George Spencer at *Poetry Thin Air* (video). He teaches literary and cultural studies at New Jersey Institute of Technology where he is a professor of English. More information and samples of his poetry and other work can be found at.
BurtKimmelman.com.

Bar Mitzvah

They stand before the ark—rabbi,
cantor, the boy between them, draped
in white prayer shawls, heads covered by
embroidered skull caps—and draw back
the curtains to reveal the scrolls

covered in their opulent sheath
of bejeweled dark felt cloth, red
and blue stones held in place as if
by a deep night. While the one sings,
the other, a tall man, reaches
in and lifts the hidden text, the
sacred law, onto his shoulder,

and they come among us, we who
touch the living Torah with our
books of prayer or silken tassels,
and then touch our lips to seal our
pact with the invisible God.

The three of them return to where
they began, and the boy, looking
into the rabbi's eyes, takes the
scripture from his arms, and staggers
for a brief moment under the
heavy weight, steadying himself,
while this man removes its cover,

and then they, together, settle
it on the podium so it
might be unrolled to the proper
spot, as the cantor ends his prayer.
The rabbi takes up the silver

cursor and directs the boy to
where he must begin, and so the
boy intones his bare entreaties
until the moment when the small
children run up behind him to
shower him with bags of candy.
At this instant he is a man.

Mikvah, **Warsaw Ghetto 1941**
    At a screening of An Unfinished Film, *New York City 2010*

They wade into the
water, naked, in
silence, shoulders hunched
over, in their fear
betraying the lens.

There are dark splotches
in the celluloid
where their groins were and
where the soldiers, out
of the frame, could aim.

In far off Berlin
an information
officer realized
what he was seeing,
hid it in a vault.

A young girl in the
ghetto who, by luck,
has become an old
woman, is being
shown the restored film.

Watching the haggard
bodies, the clumsy
attempts to obey,
she sighs, as if she
has to be polite.

"When the Germans showed
up there was always
trouble," she says, the
fact of the matter
unalterable.

Bruce Lader

Born in New York City in 1946, he is the author of six books, including *Embrace* and *Landscapes of Longing*. *Discovering Mortality* was a finalist for the 2006 Brockman-Campbell Book Award. His poems have appeared in *Poetry, New York Quarterly, New Millennium Writings, Fulcrum*, and other magazines and anthologies. Winner of the 2010 Left Coast Eisteddfod Poetry Competition, he has received a writer-in-residence fellowship from The Wurlitzer Foundation and an honorarium from the College of Creative Studies at UC-Santa Barbara.
www.BruceLader.com

Ode to Klezmer Musicians

They fiddled ecstatic legacies of life
to a universe that didn't seem to notice saxophones of joy
resound like ram's horns in synagogues of the soul.

Tyrants ordered police to silence the birds of fire,
yet they wandered with their poetry and singing
to childbirths, Bar Mitzvahs, weddings, funerals,

like Gypsies tossed a kopek, given a bowl of soup,
shtetl to shtetl in Eastern Europe, Russia, the 1800s,
labeled riffraff by officials for trumpeting

Yiddish songs and Hasidic prayers.
Taxed to beggarhood by loaded administrators
who stole off to hear them for nothing,

the outlaws proudly offered their extravagance,
sorrowful chants that journeyed through clarinets
and trombones, transformed into festivals of hope.

The minstrels didn't know their blacklisted music
that can lift despondent spirits to euphoria
would meld with New Orleans jazz and Brazilian samba,

melodies bridge over the abyss of the Holocaust,
percussion pulsing dance rhythms to the dream
of a peaceful homeland beyond obstructions to liberty.

Breaks

This pool game (the only) with my father
would be different, monopolizing Sunday
evening away from his clients' accounts.

He seemed out of practice. Three straight racks
went to me, seventeen, hands-down margins
narrowing. Then the hustler who said he hadn't

shot since his teens, said "Put your money
where your mouth is," started pocketing
combinations, my score accelerating

backwards as he bridged runs like Mosconi.
This was take-no-prisoners chess, overwhelming
offensive strategy certain as his wrestling pins

and seven-letter Scrabbles. He didn't give
an inch of allowance, targeted with sword,
I parried safeties, he gained advantage

on the table, applying subtle topspin follow
and adroit draw, manipulated me
with English. "I've seen that easy shot

missed a thousand times," he psyched
as I lined up an angle, prowled the ring
in a title bout that couldn't be stopped,

he circled and surveyed to keep the belt
and crown of his kingdom; we deployed
like rival pitchers on the battlefield

of Yankee Stadium. His legend returned,
found strike-zone corners, delivered
in extra innings like Old Reliable.

Cue chalk on nicotine-stained fingers,
he loosened collar, lit a Camel, set it
on the table-rail. Scattered the triangle.

Finessing bridge hands like Goren,
he maneuvered into position. Chips down,
a long shot balanced on the edge,

dropped. I changed the game from Straight
to Eight Ball, but he didn't leave a prayer
on the green felt; I doubled the pot

in Rotation and that shark sank winners
till I tossed in the towel, bankrupt.
"Want a rematch?" he prodded, as we left.

*

In a separate season after he died,
I puzzle out why he needed to prove himself,
fight for respect, would not be friends.

He wanted me to feel a battle he'd fought,
a child of Yiddish-speaking immigrants
growing up in a Bronx tenement without

the advantages I was wasting on billiards
bowling and girls. The merciless streets
he'd savvied didn't fancy any prima donnas,

and so you could catch worse than hell
for being an angel minding your own beeswax.
Get an iota careless and lower your guard

or neglect to keep bouncing on your toes,
you might find racetracks around eyes
set deep as a Talmudist, or brains splattered.

I wanted to flatten him, but that would have
burned like the Dodgers defeating the Yanks
in the World Series. Much stronger,

he intended to say it was absolutely copasetic
if I didn't measure up as expected,
didn't fulfill the chances he was providing

that *his* father couldn't. I would have replied
he was nonpareil, cooler than his pinochle
and horseracing buddies, a real man

who never miscued and lost control, never
messed up as a father, though the fact is
he was no contest for my scratch bowling.

I swear I wanted to kill him, and thank him
for his lasting lessons, the challenge
of transcending his proud, revenant spirit.

Joy Ladin

Born in Rochester, New York, in 1961, she is the author of five books of poetry from Sheep Meadow Press: *Alternatives to History, The Book of Anna, Transmigration, Coming to Life,* and *The Definition of Joy*. A sixth book, *Psalms*, was published by Wipf & Stock. Her memoir, *Through the Door of Life: a Jewish Journey Between Genders*, published by University of Wisconsin Press, was a 2012 National Jewish Book Award finalist. Her poems and essays have appeared in many publications and anthologies, and she is a frequent contributor to *Tikkun*. She holds the David and Ruth Gottesman Chair in English at Stern College of Yeshiva University, where she teaches writing and American literature and directs the Writing Center.

Amelioration of a Dream

> *The words in this poem were found in the ritual entitled "Amelioration of a Dream" in the* Complete Artscroll Siddur; *the sentences are my own.*

You have seen a good dream: merciful decrees, joyous laments,
    transformations – seven –
of evil into Heaven, Heaven into lips, lips into clothing, clothing into
    dying,
dying into dancing, maidens into elders, sacrilege into salvation.
The dream is good, the dream was good, good will arrive in the
    dream
and fall to the ground, eat the sun and shade the moon,
good will be your groans and your wine, your sorrow and your
    fullness. This is the dream
in which God's foot doesn't falter, God's help doesn't slumber.
In this good, this very good, dream,
you accept the goodness of those who harm you,

the good that falls like hair onto your lips,
the good that raises mountains and illuminates time, the good you
    accept
day and night, departing and arriving, in your hands and in your
    heart,
good that delights and approves and establishes
a household in your dreams where boys are singing curses that
    become blessings,
good you make known the next morning, to three good friends,
who know that goodness can be disturbing, a portent,
who know you will but haven't died,
who know the fullness of your mind, your will and your might,
the goodness you flee so it will return to you,
the goodness you eat like bread: the good dream,
the dream God dreams and God interprets,
the dream that undoes your lamentation
and says, for your sake—you are so frightened—
"You have seen a good dream."

Psalm I: 10

You like to meet me here
In the badly-lit depths
Of Café Despair

Where none of Your friends will see You
Ordering wine, squeezing my hand,
Coming on to yet another body

No one but You
Would dream of touching.
You think You might get lucky,

That I might let You in
For a glass of wine and a few sweet nothings
About how You've always loved me,

Might be desperate enough to surrender
The defenses I admit
Have never defended me from anything

But admitting
How much I need
The sleight of Your hands

Burning in my darkness
Like the candles starring
The café atmosphere

That makes us intimates, intimating
Favors to be granted,
Though from Your perspective

I'm already split
Into thighs
Of surrender and bitterness,

Already wondering in my emptied bed
If You were ever there,
Swollen with desire, and what

If any love you made
When You sowed
My void with fire.

Hank Lazer

Born in San Jose, California in 1950, he is a Professor of English at the University of Alabama. He has published 17 books of poetry, most recently *Portions, The New Spirit, Elegies & Vacations,* and *Days*. He edits the Modern and Contemporary Poetics Series for the University of Alabama Press. Author of *Opposing Poetries*, his poems and essays appear in *American Poetry Review, Boston Review,* and *Virginia Quarterly Review*. In 2008, *Lyric & Spirit: Selected Essays, 1996-2008* was published by Omnidawn. Lazer has given readings and talks throughout the U.S. and in China, the Canary Islands, Spain, Cuba, Canada, and France. Audio and video recordings—including readings from *Portions* and an interview for Art International Radio—can be found at Lazer's PennSound website: http://writing.upenn.edu/pennsound/x/Lazer.html

Torah

every day when
i arise i
carry the torah

bear it aloft
for the torch
that it is

carry it burning
& unconsumed into
the darkness of

the day unable
to find a
temple i keep

alive the memory
of the Temple
destroyed the torch

becomes the ash
the blossom of
my father's bones

David Lehman

Born in New York City in 1948, the son of Holocaust refugees, David Lehman is the author of *Yeshiva Boys, When a Woman Loves a Man, The Evening Sun, The Daily Mirror,* and *Valentine Place*, all from Scribner, as well as *Operation Memory* and *An Alternative to Speech*, both from Princeton University Press. A volume of his *New and Selected Poems* is forthcoming from Scribner. He and James Cummins collaborated on a book of sestinas, *Jim and Dave Defeat the Masked Man*; with Judith Hall he joined forces to create a book of poems and collages, *Poetry Forum*. Lehman is the editor of *The Oxford Book of American Poetry* and series editor of *The Best American Poetry* (Scribner), which he initiated in 1988. In 2010 he won ASCAP's Deems Taylor Award for his nonfiction book *A Fine Romance: Jewish Songwriters, American Songs*. He also wrote and designed the traveling exhibition based on the book, which visited fifty-five libraries in twenty-seven states in 2011 and 2012. Among Lehman's other books are a study in detective novels, a group portrait of the New York School of poets, and an account of the scandal sparked by the revelation that a Yale University eminence had written anti-Semitic and pro-Nazi articles for a leading newspaper in his native Belgium. He teaches at the New School in New York City.

God: A Sestina

God
in the splendor of his absence
cajoled argued
refused to believe
the news denied
it was a hoax.

Call off the hoax,
he said. You can't copyright God.
The judge denied
the appeal. The absence
of evidence argued
for ambiguity. Yet you believe.

In what do you believe?
In the value of a hoax.
It's as philosophers have long argued
concerning the existence of God.
The consensus is his absence
will go on. Motion to dismiss denied.

But some things can't be denied.
The inventive power of belief,
in the void left by the absence
of divinity, can hatch a hoax
overnight while the shadow of God
slips in and out of learned argument.

After hours of argument
the priests defy rather than deify,
and God
escapes the belief—
system, reduced to a hoax,
a fear of rhetoric disguising the absence

that surrounds us as if the absence
were real as air and not fake as an argument
no one wins because it was a hoax
and because the debators claimed deniability
for themselves and banishment for believers
in the old wrathful all-knowing God.

One theory: God enjoyed a clever hoax
but denied planning his absence in advance
and argued for a suspension of disbelief.

A Little History

Some people find out they are Jews.
They can't believe it.
They have always hated Jews.
As children they had roamed in gangs on winter nights in the old
 neighborhood, looking for Jews.
They were not Jewish, they were Irish.
They brandished broken bottles, tough guys with blood on their lips,
 looking for Jews.
They intercepted Jewish boys walking alone and beat them up.
Sometimes they were content to chase the Jew and he could elude
 them by running away. They were happy just to see him run
 away. The coward! All Jews were yellow.
They spelled Jew with a small j jew.
And now they find out they are Jews themselves.
It happened at the time of the Spanish Inquisition.
To escape persecution, they pretended to convert to Christianity.
They came to this country and settled in the southwest.
At some point the oral tradition failed the family, and their secret
 faith died.
No one would ever have known if not for the bones that turned up
 on the dig.
A disaster. How could it have happened to them?
They are in a state of panic—at first.
Then they realize that it is the answer to their prayers.
They hasten to the synagogue or build new ones.
They are Jews at last!
They are free to marry other Jews, and divorce them, and intermarry
 with gentiles, God forbid.
They are model citizens, clever and thrifty.
They debate the issues.
They fire off earnest letters to the editor.
They vote.
They are resented for being clever and thrifty.
They buy houses in the suburbs and agree not to talk so loud.

They look like everyone else, drive the same cars as everyone else, yet in their hearts they know they're different.
In every *minyan* there are always two or three, hated by the others, who give life to one ugly stereotype or another:
The grasping Jew with the hooked nose or the Ivy League Bolshevik who thinks he is the agent of world history.
But most of them are neither ostentatiously pious nor excessively avaricious.
How I envy them! They *believe*.
How I envy them their annual family reunion on Passover, anniversary of the exodus, when all the uncles and aunts and cousins get together.
They wonder about the heritage of Judaism they are passing along to their children.
Have they done as much as they could to keep the old embers burning?
Others lead more dramatic lives.
A few go to Israel.
One of them calls Israel "the ultimate concentration camp."
He tells Jewish jokes.
On the plane he gets tipsy, tries to seduce the stewardess.
People in the Midwest keep telling him he reminds them of Woody Allen.
He wonders what that means. I'm funny? A sort of nervous intellectual type from New York? A Jew?
Around this time somebody accuses him of not being Jewish enough.
It is said by resentful colleagues that his parents changed their name from something that sounded more Jewish.
Everything he publishes is scrutinized with reference to "the Jewish question."
It is no longer clear what is meant by that phrase.
He has already forgotten all the Yiddish he used to know, and the people of that era are dying out one after another.
The number of witnesses keeps diminishing.
Soon there will be no one left to remind the others and their children.

That is why he came to this dry place where the bones have come to life.
To live in a state of perpetual war puts a tremendous burden on the population.
As a visitor he felt he had to share that burden.
With his gift for codes and ciphers, he joined the counter-terrorism unit of army intelligence.
Contrary to what the spook novels say, he found it possible to avoid betraying either his country or his lover.
This was the life: strange bedrooms, the perfume of other men's wives.
As a spy he had a unique mission: to get his name on the front page of the nation's newspaper of record. Only by doing that would he get the message through to his immediate superior.
If he goes to jail, he will do so proudly; if they're going to hang him anyway, he'll do something worth hanging for.
In time he may get used to being the center of attention, but this was incredible:
To talk his way into being the chief suspect in the most flamboyant murder case in years!
And he was innocent!
He could prove it!
And what a book he would write when they free him from this prison:
A novel, obliquely autobiographical, set in Vienna in the twilight of the Hapsburg Empire, in the year that his mother was born.

Rika Lesser

Born in Brooklyn, New York in 1953, she is the author of four books of poetry: *Questions of Love: New & Selected Poems, Growing Back: Poems 1972-1992, All We Need of Hell,* and *Etruscan Things.* She has translated more than a dozen collections of poetry or fiction, including works by Göran Sonnevi, Gunnar Ekelöf, and Claes Andersson from the Swedish, and Rafik Schami, Rainer Maria Rilke, and Hermann Hesse from the German. Her translation of *Mozart's Third Brain* by Göran Sonnevi was a finalist for the 2010 PEN Award for Poetry in Translation. A Brooklyn native and resident educated at Yale College and Columbia University, Rika Lesser has taught poetry writing and literary translation at many places. Co-chair of its Translation Committee from 1989 to 1995, she served on the Executive Board of PEN American Center from 1989 to 1996. She makes her home in Brooklyn Heights. Her newest work, *The Brazen Plagiarist,* is a collaboration with Cecile Inglessis Margellos on a selection of poems by Greek poet Kiki Dimoula, the 2010 recipient of the European Prize for Literature. For additional information, please visit her website:
http://www.rikalesser.com

Arrival

Start the day on auto-
matic pilot as best
you can   Keep it a blur
of weather, temperature
until you take a sip
of water, rotate hip
in socket, emerge from
reverie, nightmare, pum-

melling a chest that might
have been your own at cock's
crow
        Now upright, prepare
food and drink
Hold yourself
back from yesterday's thoughts
last night's circles   Grind cin-
namon, flax seeds   Stir diced
apple into hot cereal
When the first fragrant tex-
tured spoonful returns your
small maternal grand-
father to you, you are
here

Menorah

Through tears she inspected all their lives
had been, as if they were dead together.
Nothing could wash them from her mind; they
burned like acid eating through copper.

Fluid yet fixed, trembling branches of a tall
spruce thrashing in crosswinds. A single tree
strung in the darkness with strange lights:
white, blue, and amber.

Caught in the wind their arms traced
circles: hands in prayer over lit candles.
Like her mother veiled with the sacred cloth,
she lit candles. Watched the tree burn.

Lynn Levin

Born in St. Louis, Missouri in 1953, she is a poet, writer, and literary translator, and she teaches creative writing at the University of Pennsylvania and Drexel University. She is the author of four collections of poems: *Miss Plastique*; *Fair Creatures of an Hour*, a 2010 Next Generation Indie Book Awards finalist in poetry; *Imaginarium*, a finalist for *ForeWord Magazine*'s 2005 Book of the Year Award; and *A Few Questions about Paradise*. She is the co-author of *Poems for the Writing: Prompts for Poets*.

A Misty Day on Mt. Nebo

Not that it was a cake walk,
but the way we tell the story the best
part of the journey wasn't our rediscovery
of milk and honey, but
the chase through the split
sea and trek through the red
kiln, the wandering and straying
from faith, the habit of playing
fast and loose with destruction. Together
twenty years. Even if we

are married for forty I don't
think we could ever set foot
in that historically certified
dreamhouse we promised
each other. Besides, my nerves just couldn't
take so much happiness. Though
in a deli once,
having a pastrami on rye with a slice
of pickle, I dreamed

of it. In Jordan in the parched

Mountains of Moab we stood
hand in hand that August on the top
of Mt. Nebo in backpacks and hiking boots,
our canteens brimming with sweet water
from Wadi Musa—that place in the wilderness
where Moses, breaking faith with the Lord
and furious with the tribes, struck
the rock twice bringing water
forth and his own sad end,
having come that far
only to be be forbidden

the promised land.
In that heat I considered what Heraclitus said,
that personality is fate. How,
as with Moses, anger and impetuosity
also run in our veins as does
the tendency to break
tablets, faith, engagements, doors,
and how that puts so much distance
between us
and the longed-for world.
From the summit of Nebo
I gazed over the distant bliss—
forgetting for a moment the dung
of the sheep that gave the milk,
the buzz of the bees
about the honey. Khaled, our

Palestinian guide, led us up
so that we could look out like Moses
over the land, but
there was a mist. All
I could make out was the black snake
of the Jordan, the fringe of Jericho,

the Salt Sea that shone like a lead
mirror in the air that exerted
so much pressure. Somewhere in the haze
hid the city, which just
for that moment I believed
was a place of peace. then I wondered

what if the Absent-Minded One, Blessed be He,
had accidentally scheduled
a misty day to show Moses
all that he suffered for, but which
could never be his.
So I just imagined the haven, which,
if you were of a mystical turn, you might
call my personal Jerusalem—bright
purpose each morning, ecstasy
each night, endless
patience, with the children, rich
dark coffee with steamed
milk, a little plate of
sesame candy made with honey, peace
in the house, courage,
work, friends, and this
I wish, my love, with you beside me
in the wilderness.

Eve and Lilith Go to Macy's

In the fitting room at Macy's
Eve shimmies into a pair of leopard-print leggings
then mocks a dance pose.
"OMG! You're hotter than a habanero in those pants,"
gasps Lilith. She slides her finger
down Eve's shapely hip
as though striking a match
then blows out her finger.

Eve can't believe how good that feels
through the cotton-polyester-spandex blend.
Lilith always went for men in a big way
but maybe the oversexed act
was overcompensation, a put-on.
Maybe Lilith is gay.
Maybe *I'm* gay, thinks Eve
wishing her friend would touch her again.

In the Macy's fitting room
with the triple-paneled mirror
the women's figures mingle and multiply.
Looking at one of her selves
Eve moves her right arm
but in the mirror it looks like her left arm.
She can't be sure which image
reflects the real Eve.

In the champagne of the moment
she turns to Lilith, the real one, the warm one
intending to bestow upon her
an air kiss of gratitude
at most a smooch on the cheek,

but Lilith catches Eve's mouth,
draws her to her other self.
Eve can't remember

when she's ever had a kiss like that.
Maybe she never has, never will again
so what is the point in stopping?

The women linger in each other's arms
as the hidden security camera
looks on with its mysterious eye.
And the women are okay with that.
They know that eye sees all things.
Sees all. Says nothing.

Jeffrey Levine

Born in Washington, DC in 1949, he is the author of three books of poetry: *Rumor of Cortez*, nominated for a 2006 *Los Angeles Times* Literary Award in Poetry, and *Mortal, Everlasting*, which won the 2002 Transcontinental Poetry Prize. The third book, *Jubilo*, will be published in 2013. His many poetry prizes include the Larry Levis Prize from the *Missouri Review*, the James Hearst Poetry Prize from *North American Review*, the *Mississippi Review* Poetry Prize, the *Ekphrasis* Poetry Prize, and the *American Literary Review* poetry prize. A graduate of the Warren Wilson MFA Program for Writers, Levine is founder, Editor-in-Chief and Publisher of Tupelo Press, an award-winning independent literary press located in the historic Eclipse Mill in the Berkshire Mountains of Western Massachusetts. In addition, Levine serves on the core faculty of the Colrain Manuscript Conferences. He blogs at: http://jeffreyelevine.com

Mazurka

I was selling tulip bulbs smuggled in from Holland.
A kind of circus in the back alleys, past
lime-white cottages with thatched roofs below Bratislava,
mellow peaches on the trees in the reddish-yellow approach
of summer evening. Peony Tulip Angeliques, Marvel and Obdam
Narcissus, the rare Praestans Fusilier, Darwin Snow Peaks.

Of these tulips—so profound, serenity
I've learned to say in five languages, seven dialects.
I could say other things by memory:
Perhaps the electron is neither particle nor wave,
but grief instead, a dissonance, less simple.

This I say in English, the tulips go even faster.
Next to me a peasant hawked his oblong, blue-black eggs.
Music frightens the oxen, he said, in Czech.
And then in English, the single word, "pathetic,"
his accent in all three syllables like a relief map
of pressure zones and granite.

He hummed an old mazurka to his even older horse,
damp nostrils trembling, flanks sweating
manganese and iron oxide, odor of subterranean stone,
while I fed the roan bulb after bulb from my open palm.

The Herbalist

Next life, I'll devote to the earnest pursuit of languor.
A dubious sort, I'll live like a Buddha, impervious, fat.
What a relief to flout unknowable accounts—
let the earth offer up its sober charities if it wants.
Moses strikes the rock and brings forth the bubbling stream.
We get to swim in it, lie down in it, do what we want.
Want. The thing unfurls like tight-packed knots
of fiddlehead fern, mandrakes, gentian, garden spurge,
opening large upon themselves, stopless, filling the sky.
Let whatever we find turn to seeds, jackbeans, stalks
uplifted, rattle like brittlebush in a dry wind while years lock
into years, and contentment fills my mouth.

Julia B. Levine

Born in New York City in 1958, she has recently published her latest poetry collection, *Ditch-tender*, through University of Tampa Press. Her awards include the University of Tampa Prize for her second collection, *Ask*, the Anhinga Prize and a bronze medal from *Foreword Magazine* for her first collection, *Practicing for Heaven*, The Discovery/*The Nation* award, the Pablo Neruda Prize in poetry, and multiple Pushcart Prize nominations. Her work has been anthologized in several collections, including *The Places That Inhabit Us*, and *The Autumn House Anthology of Contemporary American Poetry*.

Angels

A strange barking sounds from the long mast of geese.
How slow the forest in winter, all day
only a handful of dead branches
falling gently down
around this lake. And how fairly snow
seeks out the bones of each pine,
spanning across the uneven ground like sleep,
while something hovers just beyond sensation.

This stillness
must be a kind of music:
a couple staring out at sun
burning from the basin's rim,
the young woman
letting newspaper float from her hands,
a dog turning back
where the pier has buckled. It has been several months

since the catamarans swelled with wind, a moment
suddenly drawing me forward
into the question of God.

Then I did not know
grief can only learn a shoreline.

And I had not yet seen
this sky entering each black-winged bird
as it climbed out of dark water
into the mercy of so much light.

Windstorm on the Marsh

We lie beside the drowning grass,
willows groaning

as they are torn apart,
tire tracks

swept clean of dust
and lifted up like bones.

It's hard, love, always
coming into something else,

and this is how we'll go,
isn't it,

back to where the geese
drag beneath this sky,

the loons
pulled down to silence,

a wordless rushing
over water.

Back to where the pintails
thrown up in flocks,

are thrown back in pairs.
How hard they work

to split their wings
against the gusts, and still

the ducks are dropping
in a wild salt of dark,

in the mated hands of God
that will break us

back to one.
Hardest,

where I love you most,
how we touch

beneath the emptied lanterns
of the rushes

and watch the shaken sky.

Eighteen Days of Fog and Rain

i.

A trapeze of seabirds
Dips across the Pacific's graveyard.

Slender flutes of white
Torpedo into the future's accident.

And who can resis stepping into the tidal madness
Of narcissus, snowbells, pale daffodils,

Believing love for one thing
Might bring another back?

Believing these starry brooms
Nosing up through the underworld,

Are the bog's ecstatic argument
With the poet I read last night, lamenting

I wish God were not inside me.

ii.

As if death were not itself a meaning,
Our children want to hear the story

Again, of the vanished that return:
The boy the mother cannot hold

Against the tsunami's suck,
Though later the father finds him

Clinging to a tree, an upturned boat.
Alive. Dead. It's not the boy who matters,

But the telling, everyone leaning forward
Into their own original scars:

Love and desolation
A constant undertow

To the exhausted breath
Of time

iii.

If we have to die to begin again;
If we must learn to let go

Of each other more easily;
Is it sadness or awe, I feel then,

Watching my youngest carry her chickens
Over the flooded pond?

And there, at the edges,
I can see my child moving deeper

Into the volatile perfume
Of flesh and rain.

Yes, say it is possible:

The silent clock of being
Shutters and opens all at once.

Say she has to touch it for herself—
The long threads of faith

We swing from—
And so she drops her flock

One by one—Yes,
Say those startled, stupid birds

Fall
Beyond such useless wings.

Rachel Loden

Born in Washington, DC in 1948, she is the author of *Dick of the Dead*, shortlisted for both the PEN USA Literary Award for Poetry and the California Book Award. Her first book, *Hotel Imperium*, won the Contemporary Poetry Series competition and was selected as one of the ten best poetry books of the year by the *San Francisco Chronicle*. Her work has appeared in the *Washington Post*'s "Poet's Choice" column and the Best American Poetry series. She is the recipient of a Pushcart Prize and a Fellowship in Poetry from the California Arts Council.

Cape Disappointment

Obsession v. Dementia: which will win?
If I forget thee, O Jerusalem,

It will be like walking into the next room
To look for the messiah

And then walking out again. Sometimes
I think I have forgotten

What I most earnestly wanted to forget
And that's when I am reminded

Of my tenure in exile here
At Cape Disappointment. I didn't choose

To ply my song trade in this sorrowscape
But such was my ridiculous fate.

Kiss-Cucumber, Schatzie, please look
And see whether I left my harp out on

The willows of Babylon. If I do not
Remember thee, if I do not prefer thee

Zion to my chief joy, let me
Lick honey off the letters of your name.

What the Gravedigger Needs
   Teuva, Finland

overalls
rubber boots
leather gloves
iron spear to loosen up the frozen ground
lantern
spade
length of rope
board to prevent mourners falling in
bicycle to go from grave to grave

Rachel Malis

Born in Bridgeport, Connecticut in 1985, she earned her MFA from Arizona State University in 2010. She was a runner up in 2009's Slapering Hol chapbook contest via the Hudson Valley Writers' Center. Rachel has been published in the *New Mexico Poetry Review*, *Adirondack Review*, *Superstition Review*, and several others. While completing her masters degree, Rachel received awards and a grant to travel to Ukraine, the Czech Republic, and Australia. She has poetry in a forthcoming women's anthology called *The Moment I Knew: Reflections from Women on Life's Defining Moments*.

Ewe Translations

The snake, lying in the road
is unable to move for his bloat.
Even the skin over its nose
has been stretched taut
over the ribs of the sheep,
whose skin is taut over the ewe
in her belly. In Hebrew, ewe
means Rachel, as in little lamb,
virginal wool, growing inside
in curls, like moss. I feel this sometimes.
Not the bloat of the snake,
but the dark pressure of being
the thing inside. The snake, eventually,
must be drugged and dragged
out of the road. The effort of this
leaves him unsettled, and after all
that bearing down and swallowing,
he regurgitates the sheep,
almost still whole. Here, a hoof,
a shank, the small lamb's lost bleat.

Sandra Cohen Margulius

Born in Milwaukee, Wisconsin in 1950, her poem "Women and Birds" was selected as the 2005 winner in *RUNES*. Her work has also appeared in *The Cream City Review, Radiance Magazine, Hodge Podge Poetry, Women Writing, Buffalo Bones, Robin's Next, Laughing Boy,* and *Sparkle, Sizzle, Hiss.* She completed her MA in Creative Writing in December, 2001 at the University of Wisconsin-Milwaukee. She is a mother of three grown children and grandmother of Eli, Jonah, and Rayna Kaufman, and Spencer Margulius. She continues to live and write in Bayside, Wisconsin with her husband, Simon.

Repeating
dedicated to Gertrude Stein

Oh Gertrude, Jew sister, master of repetition, repeating
repeating completing sentences sentences with no meaning
no meaning. I have no meaning. What did you mean? Did you mean
to say nothing? I say nothing. He hears nothing. Nothing he hears
yet I talk I talk I talk and say nothing. He hears nothing but talk
and repeating repeating the same words the same words. He
hears nothing of my words my words are nothing. My words say
nothing my words are not heard not heard my words repeating
    repeating
and beating my head against walls against walls like talking to
my mother my mother who hears nothing nothing like he who
hears nothing when I talk and talk and repeat and he won't hear
what I say. What I say means nothing to him. He can't hear my
words my words echo in my head in my head where they start
to come out to be heard by he who hears nothing says nothing.
Nothing I say is important. Get to the point. Get to the point.
What is the point? I don't know the point or I wouldn't
keep talking keep talking, talking so you will hear me hear me

hear my words echoing in my own ears that hears only myself
talking, talking to he who hears nothing. My mouth opening and
   shutting
open and speaking, speaking the words that he doesn't hear
the words that repeat and repeat so he will listen
so he will hear me. Never hears me never listens to words
that I want him to hear, words that open me, words that spill me
spill me spill me into him so he will finally listen to hear who I am,
who I am, who am I? I am who? Who am I that he can't hear me,
my words that spill unto and into and over him like
a waterfall of blue words that will drown him blue words
that spill wet from my mouth so that he will listen
and validate and validate and validate that I am who I am.
Who am I if he can't validate who I am, then what is the point of my
talking and talking and spilling and spilling my words
telling him who I am. Who am I if he won't listen won't listen
listen to who I am?
Who am I?

Liat Mayer

Born in Milwaukee in 1984, she lived in Israel for some time as a child and teenager. She lives currently in Oakland, California. Her work has been published in *Gangs Love You*, *Molochide Templon*, and *Fishwrap*.

Jerusalem Desert

The city is narrow this evening—

every white stone is another word
called to you. The shape
of your name fills my mouth—

knowing that every way to you
is blocked there is a thin
quiet in the air.

If only the dust
knew ways to arrive.

Again and again we return
alone and still we have not met.

Ben Mazer

Born New York City in 1964, he studied with Seamus Heaney and William Alfred at Harvard, as well as with Christopher Ricks, Geoffrey Hill, and Archie Burnett at the Editorial Institute, Boston University. His collections of poems include *Poems, January 2008*, and *White Cities*. Editor of *Selected Poems of Frederick Goddard Tuckerman*, Landis Everson's *Everything Preserved: Poems 1955-2005*, and an edition of the poems of John Crowe Ransom. He is also a contributing editor to *Fulcrum: an Annual of Poetry and Aesthetics*.

Epilogue

It is youth that understands old age
and your repulsion is but a projection
an image of the loathing you obtain.
I've seen the fall come in and think I shall
follow each leaf that winds about the house
to where you stutter, the end of the tether
where grace walks through the bridal foliage
and no one could mistake you for another.
After that, they are only leaves to burn.
And when the flowers burst upon the rain
the roofs shall keep their solemn gentle witness
far from the young men who travel far
to fill their noses with the autumn air.
Daybreak is decent as awakening.
And love is gentle, though he is no scholar.
What if I filled my notebook with his words
sketched suddenly with no least hesitation
would she return to him when it came fall
or would she sink into a bitter winter
not even counting the blossoms that are gone.

How many times the autumn rain recurs
to wind about the river in the evening
or fall like one great ocean in the dawn.
No matter, he has had enough of her
and leaves his youth in hope of something better.
A drop expresses all the flooding water,
the wind instills the trees with sentiment,
and no one, no one can reverse the patter
of the darkness that's enclosed within.
It stares across the city in the dawn
and cannot wake these shrouds of memory.

Colleen McKee

Born in the Ozarks in Missouri in 1974, her most recent book is *9 Kinds of Wrong*. She is also the author of the chapbooks *My Hot Little Tomato*, and *A Partial List of Things I Have Done for Money*. Additionally, she is co-editor of the anthology *Are We Feeling Better Yet? Women Speak About Health Care in America*. She lives in Oakland, California and teaches at the Academy of Art in San Francisco. http://colleenmckee.blogspot.com

Taschlikh

By the wizened roots of a massive oak
under the juniper tree

I cast my sins into the creek
scraping the lint from my pocket,

a mass of gritty regrets
tangled together, lodging under my nails.

I sat on the muddy bank
not caring about my skirt.

Blue gentians twisted in the oak roots,
clover bent under my boots.

One bit of foil was clumped in with my sins.
The lint swished downstream,

but the tiny glint of foil,
flashing in the sun, hooked

on a mass of gingko leaves too great
to be moved by mere water.

Some sins are too beautiful
to ever let go.

Erika Meitner

Born in Queens, New York in 1975, she is the author of three books of poems: *Inventory at the All-night Drugstore*, winner of the 2002 Anhinga Prize for Poetry; *Ideal Cities*, a 2009 National Poetry Series winner; and *Makeshift Instructions for Vigilant Girls*. Her poems have appeared in publications including *The New Republic, Virginia Quarterly Review, APR, Tin House, Best American Poetry 2011,* and elsewhere. Meitner is a first-generation American: her father is from Haifa, Israel; her mother was born in Stuttgart, Germany, which is where her maternal grandparents settled after surviving Auschwitz, Ravensbruck, and Mauthausen concentration camps. She is currently an associate professor of English at Virginia Tech, where she teaches in the MFA program.

Yiddishland

The people who sang to their children in Yiddish and worked in Yiddish
and made love in Yiddish are nearly all gone. Phantasmic. Heym.

Der may kumt shoyn on. The month of May has arrived. At the cemetery
my aunt has already draped my grandmother's half of the tombstone

with a white sheet. The fabric is tacked to the polished granite
by grey and brown rocks lifted from my grandfather's side of the plot.

He's been gone over twenty-five years. We are in Beth Israel Cemetery,
Block 50, Woodbridge, New Jersey for the unveiling and the sky is like lead.

We are in my grandmother's shtetl in Poland, but everyone is dead.
The Fraternal Order of Bendin-Sosnowicer Sick & Benevolent Society

has kept these plots faithfully next to their holocaust memorial—
grey stone archway topped with a menorah and a curse: *Pour out Thy wrath*

upon the Nazis and the wicked Germans for they have destroyed the seed of Jacob.
May the almighty avenge their blood. Great is our sorrow, and no consolation is to be found!

My sister, in her cardboard kippah, opens her prayer book—a special edition
she borrowed from rabbinical school—and begins to read in Aramaic.

No one can bring themselves to personalize the fixed liturgy, say anything additional.
My son is squatting at the grave next to us, collecting decorative stones

from the Glickstein's double plot. We eat yellow sponge cake and drink
small cups of brandy to celebrate my grandmother's life. We are no longer mourners,

says Jewish law. Can we tell this story in Yiddish? Put the words in the right places?
My son cracks a plastic cup until it's shredded to strips, looks like a clear spider,

sounds like an error. When my sister finally pulls back the sheet, all the things
my grandmother was barely fit on the face of the marker. A year ago at the funeral,

her friend Goldie told me she was strong like steel, soft like butter—
women like that

they don't make any more. My mother tries to show my
grandmother—now this grey marker—

my son, how he's grown, but he squirms from her arms. *Ihr gvure iz
nit tzu beshraiben.*
Her strength was beyond description. The people who sang to their
children in Yiddish

and admonished them in Yiddish are nearly all gone, whole vanished
towns that exist now
only in books, their maps drawn entirely by heart: this unknown
continent, this language

of nowhere, these stones from a land that never was. *Der may kumt
shoyn on.*
The month of May has arrived. *Der vind voyet.* The wind howls,

says I'm not a stranger anywhere. On the stones we write all we
remember,
but we are poor guardians of memory. Can you say it in Yiddish?
Can you bless us?

Advice

Yiddish proverbs my grandmother told me
ranged from humorous to enigmatic:
Shrouds are made without pockets—one of three

and bad or good, things always come in threes—
red ribbons to ward off the evil eye.
Yiddish proverbs my grandmother gave me:

The heart is half a prophet, over tea,
saying, *I want to dance on your wedding,*
but *shrouds are made without pockets*—we'll see

*If I should live so long, God willing, I'll be
alive and you'll walk down the aisle soon.*
Yiddish proverbs my grandmother told me:

if God were living on earth now—you'll see—
people would break his windows, God forbid.
Shrouds are made without pockets, and how free

you are. I was your age in the camps; it was '43—
from the ghetto we couldn't take anything.
Yiddish stories my grandmother told me

about suitcases—*They shot a whole family*
who wouldn't let go of their possessions
        on the way to Auschwitz.
The proverb my Yiddish grandmother gave me:
Shrouds are made without pockets.

Mary Meriam

Born in Passaic, New Jersey in 1955, she has published essays, reviews, and poems appearing recently in *The New York Times, Poetry Foundation, American Life in Poetry, Measure, Mezzo Cammin, Bridges, Light, Think,* and *Sentence.* She is the author of three poetry chapbooks, and the editor of *Filled with Breath: 30 Sonnets by 30 Poets* and *Lavender Review.*

The Romance of Middle Age

Now that I'm fifty, let me take my showers
at night, no light, eyes closed. And let me swim
in cover-ups. My skin's tattooed with hours
and days and decades, head to foot, and slim
is just a faded photograph. It's strange
how people look away who once would look.
I didn't know I'd undergo this change
and be the unseen cover of a book
whose plot, though swift, just keeps on getting thicker.
One reaches for the pleasures of the mind
and heart to counteract the loss of quicker
knowledge. One feels old urgencies unwind,
although I still pluck chin hairs with a tweezer,
in case I might attract another geezer.

I'm still here

I'm still here holding up the sky for you,
bawling this heart-to-heart goodbye for you.

I'm still the child who cooks the stony stew,
the chickadee who learned to fly for you.

She looks so rich, her face so fresh and new—
you're more than friends, I catch her sigh for you.

Do I sound bitter? Am I green or blue?
Don't leave again! Don't make me cry for you!

I send some poems to the *Screw Review,*
I sit around and wait and die for you.

The marvel of my muse is constant, true.
With dedicated lust, I try for you.

Stephen Paul Miller

Born in New York City in 1951, he is the author of several books including *The Seventies Now: Culture as Surveillance*, and several poetry books including *Fort Dad, Being with a Bullet, Is Boring for the Same Reason We Stayed in Vietnam, The Bee Flies in May, Skinny Eighth Avenue*, and *There's Only One God and You're Not It*. He also co-edited, with Daniel Morris, *Radical Poetics and Secular Jewish Culture*, and, with Terence Diggory, *The Scene of My Selves: New Work on New York School Poets*. His poetry has also appeared or soon will appear in *New American Writing, Best American Poetry, Zeek, Tablet, Jacket, Columbia Review, Black Clock, Mipoesias, Boundary 2, Columbia Review, American Letters and Commentary, Another Chicago Magazine, Paterson Review, Eoagh, Coconut, Zen Monster, House Organ, Brooklyn Rail*, and *Critiphoria*, which he co-edits. He is a Professor of English at St. John's University in New York City and was a Senior Fulbright Scholar at Jagiellonian University in Krakow, Poland.

Monotheism

> broadened,
> married to itself, deeply alone
> perhaps but not.

There's Only One God And You're Not It

All the peoples of all the world
        degrade one another's gods
                but Jews first think
    your gods do not exist.

    An ordinary man,
     I go with the gods who
  bring me
  but as Babylonians drag around Yahweh

        I call all concerned to say
"We're going in an entirely different direction,
all other gods *nothing*." And it's done! You
find tons of

Israelite idols until exile,
 then nearly none.
  Yahweh marks
   Israelites

    from Canaanites when Israel's
   Canaan.
  We're the un-Canaanites,
  mighty, mighty non-Canaanites

and not the Canaanites
  bleeding other Canaanites
    for the dough to buy Egyptian protection
     to bleed Canaanites

    for more protection as un-
Canaanites take to hills and
  caves, wiping out
    Canaan slowly, though sometimes violently, from within,
   part of the larger collapses of
    the Mesopotamian 'n Egyptian empires
     bookending Canaan. Canaan's almost by definition
              double backwater,
    an ecological kaleidoscope

	between what's wilderness and settled,
		naturally selecting conditions
		for a new, agrarian, fairly classless
	Israel.

How sudden's the swing
to Israel? One or two
hundred years.
	Check

	archaeological evidence
	like palace burn marks
	and chopped
	monuments, hinting

		violent overthrow
		in Hazor, more
		gradual
		power shifts elsewhere.

			Are you sure Israel
			goes that far back?
			Some doubt it,
			but it's hard to ignore

				Egyptian
				references to
				Israelites and Canaan-to-Israel
				continuity in pottery less fancy

				but made the same—a *big*
				collective fingerprint. Distinctive
			pillar homes linking families and farms,
		not guarding wealth,

	show
	Canaan
	like
Jacob

   Israel *now*.
   Israelite gods are
  Canaanite
 except

the irresistibly
  populist
    Yahweh, the guy
      walks in our courtyard—

  El's intimate identity—
  god qua god.
   Yahweh is the god, the twin gods peak
 but he's the man,

 stern yet bubbly, a bit psycho, warm,
egalitarian,
  not about fertility as much as
    his god pals and concubine—so you need the others.

    But Yahweh's for guerrilla, misfit, and dreg,
  a new take on god Yahu
  from Midian, where Moses
meets Him and He goes,

"I met Israelites before but
  they thought I was someone else."
    How awkward. If the exodus couldn't
     have happened,

    it's still the oldest, most stirring
   Hebrew tale, oddly nailing
  where they contact
Yahweh

cuz that matters more
  than what might have happened to
    brave Canaanite slaves,
     a story you recall cuz

liberation's unnatural.
You need soppy miracles glossing real ones.
Proto-Jews are incredibly serious—funny even—
about how they treat one another

but also terrified to be an other—
you come from the other
and could slip back. Classless
agrarian utopia morphs to

monarchy, though King David's self-made
and critics who make you feel like crap
about the direction the country is going
still get enshrined

in oddly secular—
ancient Hebrew having no word for "religion"—culture
tipping
Yahweh's sword

from major to minor
ev'ry time we say goodbye.
There's such an air of gore you
daven through it—Hebrew
from the Egyptian "cross"

or "across"
as in Abraham
going through

Canaan from Mesopotamia to Egypt 'n back to Canaan—
2 terminal backwaters in one—new Israelite Canaan—
a little like the 2 "cameras" (Mesopotamia and Egypt)
bleeding together on the screen to form 3D—

that little slit on the crease of the two projections—
what Hitchcock discovers in the incredible 3D-
version of *Dial M for Murder*—that
the slimmest everyday item—

a key, for instance—
is most likely to reach your face.
Hebrews swing across the universe since
you can't erase it, setting up

synagogue scales absolutely
insecure in major
or minor.
On the one hand there's the other hand.

And what's so Yahweh or the ha-way?
Am I *ever*
monotheist? Hell, I like other gods.
I know God does.

So what's with the Book of Judges,
no, I mean Psalms going "all the
gods of all peoples
of all the nations are *NOTHING*"?

Plato might
pick up on this "your reality's false" gizmo
pulling the rug on the obvious,
giving reason the place of Yahweh over

divine family romance & poetry.
Later, Greek Jews like Philo
of Alexandria translate
iconoclasm and monotheism

onto
one
operational
plane or platform or ground
softening
monotheism,
opening it
a little,

                    inviting
                    you in
and centuries and centuries later—now—
we want everyone

monotheist so we know they
play in our
world.
  If you worship many gods

  slobs think you're a snob,
  snobs think you're a slob
  so the Japanese, for instance,
  partly to avoid

   looking like children, after
   Admiral Perry,
   prop their emperor to
   hide their gods.

    You're okay as long
    as you believe in one
    god and since
    there's only one god

     it has to be the same
     God—NOT—but that's
     okay with God who
     is also other gods.

      Huh? God's with us, not you—
      he works through you,
    Cyrus, to take us back to Jerusalem
    proving Y---- great,

   and *that's* when we *really* toss our idols
    'n go mono. We're Persian puppets maybe
      but ONE GOD keeps us together in this really together
       identity. The word

"identity" later comes from Latin for over and over and over as
if carrying over from ancient Israel.
Jewish identity
makes no sense but pops and pops and pops like Hitchcock's 3D key.

Israelites
issue from the first known peasant revolt,
but, some 700 years later, does that matter?
Yes! That's why they are first to

make all kinds of excuses for a loser god!
Would you worship a loser god? A loser can't be God!
But Yahweh long ago squares and squares
the 60s to another higher power AND

the first Israelites have a wtf what a moment
feeling
stunningly new,
assuming another name, 'n

if Israeling, so to speak,
means "wrestling
with El,"
do Yahweh 'n El

make all WWF? Don't know, probably not,
but
consensus is
founding Israelites

skip government
a century or two
for extended family settlements,
fewer than 300 people each, and

connected only by a loose council
of tough judges—
proto-Israelites
more like Thomas Jefferson than the Tea Party

since Tom's anti-government and progressive, progressive cuz
government's only for the powerful then
and Jefferson and the Israelites limit gov
   for reasons leading FDR to revive Jefferson

  as his great precursor, and Roosevelt
    consciously reclaims religious high
ground through Hillel's and Jesus's Israelite oral identities. Global
   trade through Israel troubles

the dirt poor Utopia
into adding towns, cities, and
a monarchy Yahweh's heard
  reluctantly to allow

   —and the
   bible records
   how begrudgingly
   he gives in.

Saul's a bum, David offs a guy to get his wife, Solomon don't ask.
The temple, more than Vatican, is
White House, Supreme Court, but
  not Congress cuz laws are still unwritten.

Concentrating wealth and power, the temple is the treasury and
                         Isaiah disparages kings,
              large roofs, and living off the labor
    of other Israelites.

    You
     accept temple and monarchy
     ambivalently
    if at all.

  We Israelites don't know from building a temple
   and Solomn hires foreigners, but,
  right before the Babylonian tidal wave,
  temple leaders—just at the moment they *know* I won't die for no
temple,

no monarchy, no government--find what Moses really wrote.
It was under something they had to move
while restoring the temple. Who knew
Israel né Jacob sees there'll be a temple and what's more

it'll be the one place Yahweh will accept
your livestock—YOUR
ONE
avenue to HIM,
prayer still nothing much, and in the lost scroll
Yahweh calls all other gods less than doody—
go to their shrines 'n temples and you BETTER
duck.

Idols? Covenant breakers!!!
DON'T EVEN
SPEAK Yahweh's name. I forgot!
I mean you have to *go* to the Temple and

then,
never mind, no more temple.
The scroll's what's really cool, where Yahweh is, so
might as well read it.

Which is easier than
making sense of it,
but trying's
cutting edge

since Yahweh's somehow
able to move from land
to land and temple to text.
Good luck, Yahweh. I love your new home.

In exile, circumcision's big.
People 'round us aren't that way

'n you have to stay what you become—
someone from ole Judah, Israel something else.

Keeping kosher and falling into Sabbath bliss
  also delightfully distinguish—
    and please do not intermarry.
      Facebook starts Harvard-exclusive then opens

    but we close
      ranks for inclusive
        ideological identity—get edgy
            to stay open.

          I know they're
      full of it
  but
when Yahweh

    cons Persia into conquering
      Babylon and letting us back
      I'm a believer. There's only one god.

      Stick with Yahweh. Enjoy
        His touching if psychotic collective cognitive
        shift of
        ground from which we think—

power and reality rumble in subtle, pre-Platonic spheres. You
                                Yahweh
                        sanction sweet
            proto-ideological me and mine.

        Your figure in the text orients us
          like Japan opening west
          reordering itself around the emperor—
      making him God to show

    a face of unified strength to the outside world.
        They go along to get along. Believing in many
          gods is okay among themselves
            but infantile to the West.

The Japanese aren't monotheist
and neither are we, handy as monotheism is.
One god sweeps the others
in a dustpan and walks away deist-style

so we're all cool
'n study what he left.
Computers hang on
God's trickster

track connecting all computable operations.
Another god can't come out of nowhere.
The culty Enigma code
changes

every day, but each day monotheism
reasserts itself and
wins World War II.
Monotheism

everything
not only itself,
it's nice to be a monotheist—
one god, one people, one person—

but God has no friends,
it's boring without
figure-ground excitement
sustaining on and off again oneness, i.e.,

Jewish
culture,
the pivot every
Westerner

has to make
to the accident-in-reverse
we come from—
the Midian of Deuteronomy—

giving up on teenage
drama for Shakespearean
soliloquy. Who are you talkin'?
Even

Jews go back
cuz they left
something.
Like Odysseus,

Moses returns
not as Moses
but many Moseses,
Moses descending a staircase.

Berlin goes through Jerusalem—Irving Berlin that is cuz
what cantors like Berlin's
and Harold Arlen's dads
sing really does go way back back back to ancient Israel.

The people of the book didn't notate music so
"To remember the music…melodic fragments
recur over and over…as good a working
definition of Jewish music as any" (15-16),

says Jack Gottlieb in his Smithsonian book.
In Ashkenaz tradition especially these
melodies
direct movement and life.

According to page 47
of Wilfred Sheed's *The House that George Built*,
whenever George Gershwin plays "Rhapsody in Blue,"
his father says, "Again? The 'Rhapsody'?"

Musicologist Margaret Nabarro
hears affinities 'tween her sense of ancient Israelite vocals
'n Yemenite Lembas music
so DNA researchers check Lemba

accounts of leaving sixth century B.C.E.
Israel's northern kingdom and yes they did
and I hear something similar
in "Again? The 'Rhapsody'?"

Its propositional logic—the
"on the one hand there's the other hand"—
from Greek propositional logic embedded
in Talmudic reasoning and, before that
biblical parallelism and much later
    languages like Yiddish.
Sure Yiddish comes from mediaeval German.
The point is, like proto-Israelite identity,

    it's creatively inclusive,
closed but still adjusting
as a kinda craft for cultural scanning,
adaption, dynamic blending, bleeding.

2 reasons Yiddish music sets the table for songs now:
first, Kern, Berlin, Gershwin assimilate
the swinging raga-like
variously stressed word pops and ground-altering endless

major/minor shuttles of ancient Israelite music
into mainstream Western music
for the first time since Gregorian Chants.
And, two, this music

mixes fine with other marginalized music
popping a mainstream out of the mainstream.
 "In his constant shifting from major to minor keys"
 Cole Porter "consciously wrote Jewish melodies" (191),

  says Jack Gottlieb.
Richard Rodgers and Yip Harburg are surprisingly
  intent on Porter admitting his Jewish debt
    though Porter makes no secret Irving Berlin's his man—

    Berlin writes words and music too.
      Rodgers writes music
  so Jerome Kern's
his avatar.

   Berlin looks up to George M. Cohan so
  it's not ALL about being Jewish—
  No! Cohan's not Jewish of course
though a friend thought he was

so I had to look it up
and his wife was partly Jewish,
   but I never say it is about being Jewish,
    just hard to avoid and

radical as in a root of much
culture, art, and poetry.
Yahweh's the top,
but I'm a flop of

  infinite grammatical equivalences,
   and Rodgers
    feels Porter
   hides too much,

    singling out "Night and Day,"
     "Begin the Beguine," "Love for Sale,"
     "I Love Paris," and "My Heart Belongs to Daddy"
    as Porter's greatest *and* most Jewish pieces.

   Harburg and Rodgers report what Cole tells them
    to prove how consciously Cole adapts
     Yiddish and East European
      synagogue tonal shifts and syncopations.

   Porter says he needs to base his
    music on that music
     to write his version of this fine
      and humorous

new American music.
 I don't know anything about music
  but feel God's favorite poetry
   is fine and humorous, and

    before it ever occurs to me
     Jerome Kern might
      be Jewish
       I can't get over

        how songs don't
         sound like songs
          before him, but
           the divide's Berlin's

      1911 "Alexander's Ragtime Band," "the first
       real American musical work," raves George
      Gershwin. Porter's labeled *the* great *non*-Jewish
American songbook writer—but what about Johnny

   Mercer?—though he's younger and collaborates
     so much with Arlen and other Jewish
       songwriters, but there are other brilliant
        non-Jewish twenties and thirties

     songwriters such as Ellington
      and a plethora of other African Americans,
       yet I hear what riles Rodgers and Harburg.
 Not only does Jewish culture

   influence popular music,
      it makes it what it is, a jazzier
       take on the punk pogo,
    davening

   as you glide.
    It might be a one-god world
   but Jewish culture's always shifting
 from minor to major to

      minor to major
        before you can crack the code of wherever the hell
        you are.
      When the 19th century empire of poetic form
      goes under,

    poets emigrate to Whitman—
      Irving Berlin and Cole Porter in one—
    or *really* Whitman is Moses—
    as important as it is

  to Freud that Moses be Egyptian *not*
Jewish since Freudian Moses needs
  a good murdering
  to be mourned, celebrated, eaten,

and postdated by the
temple hierarchy.
Before the temple burns,
the ten commandments

being found
miraculously
makes
Josiah cry at what a bad ass

  Moses—Deuteronomy Moses—is.
  And when the temple
    smokes
      Moses is reborn.

    Similarly, poets Whitman
      inspires right
        off don't carry Whitman to us.
          His greatest influence is indirect.

      He needs to be ignored
        before permeating
          poetry.

>   Through Whitman
>   biblical forms—
>   the nonstop melodies
>   in just talking—
>   spread by whatever structure works.

Even a secular Jew like Richard Rodgers calls out Cole
for not talking up going to school on Yiddish music.
Ironically, Rodgers outs Porter
by calling him the greatest Jewish songwriter,

though Porter did say it's necessary for a songwriter
to learn Yiddish music. I can see how Cole might be miffed.
He studies lots of musical traditions. Yet it's moot.
>   There's something

more important than say Harold Arlen praying
"Paper Moon" to friends to show it note for note a synagogue
song he probably heard from his cantor dad.
You don't need to be Jewish to write

"Fly Me to the Moon, In Other Words"
ancient Israelite/Jewish identity's built to
blend, then close, then blend
and blend cuz, first,

Israelite and Yiddish music aren't diatonic and
mix with African influences
that aren't either. All contain
western music like a cup.

Michael Rogin notes Jews absorbing
black 'n other minority American influence.
Israel Baline might use Irving Berlin as his pen name right
after writing one of his early "German" songs,

as the Nazi guard in Billy Wilder's
Stalag 17 suspects (Billy's German Jewish 'n Berlin's Russian).
I don't know music but I always thought songs don't sound right
till Jerome Kern, and I didn't even know he was Jewish.

Lots of people feel that way
about poems and American poetry at least before Whitman.
When poetic form disintegrates,
    poets drift to Walt.

 From biblical poetry he culls
something much like what Adele Berlin calls
the dueling parallel structures of
   a biblical dynamic:

A "whose making love to your old lady while you were out making
love?" dynamite in dynamic tension with biblical structure
blasting away meters no one remembers, revealing
myriads of poetic oppositions prancing like gazelles.

As Martin Luther sets time back to ancient Israel
so Whitman has nowhere else to base his
everything old new again poems-
as-one-poem; WW's USA

strings Yahweh through a public sphere,
pouring anything in it through various sifters. You
   use the Civil War,
 then Prufrock, suppressed

"Objects" that whisper and sing,
a hurtling convex mirror, Second Avenue,
a poem that talks.
 Yahweh likes his house where

   classical rhythms
    coalesce around
     intensely
radical planets,

     spreading degree zero
    talk
     in Yahweh's most intimate
      public address, talk talking 'round

      linguistically pointy
reflexive
  referential cakes and curves
    writing

        exquisitely makeshift
          grammatically parallel improv,
            syncopated logos
              pulling rabbits,

                    neurotically
                    close-
                     to-the-vest
                     redistributions of relaxed

                          poetic emphases—
                        hallmarks of
                          how Jews succeed in modern poetry
                            without even being there.

Jerry Mirskin

Born in Bronx, New York in 1953, his recent work is mostly in prose poem form—nearly "concise literary nonfiction." His second collection is *In Flagrante Delicto*. His first full-length collection, *Picture a Gate Hanging Open and Let that Gate be the Sun*, won the Mammoth Books Prize for poetry. He is currently an Associate Professor at Ithaca College and teaches select courses at Cornell University. He lives in Ithaca, New York with his wife, Wendy Dann, a theatrical director, and his son, Noah.
http://www.jerrymirskin.us

Icarus

To understand this story
you have to picture a gate hanging open
and let that gate be the sun.
Then picture a boy bursting from the spell
of too much dark, how he tumbles
and slips from the effortless grip of the clouds.
What seemed last night like a good idea,
spanking the water.
I don't really understand why he had to die
beyond understanding the statute of limitations—
how imagination goes unsupported in the sky.
I suppose I understand how water goes on living,
while people like you and me prophesy a kind of patience
a pride in flying low, a wisdom
in the plain joy of just walking around.
But, to really understand this story
you have to imagine a kind of castle loneliness.
Nights when there is no telling
from all the things that men do, just what we want to do.
From that flightless dark

it is just a small step to seeing any sign of sun
as the kind of beauty our knowing can embrace.
Maybe it is just youthful infatuation,
but who wouldn't open their arms?
Who wouldn't feel in the light of such knowledge
like putting on their wings and going out?
Picture a gate hanging open.
And let that gate be the sun.

Rock and Water

They were a perfect pair.
The boy hunched over near the rocks.
His shadow moving gently on the surface
as if he were stirring the water.
When you looked closer, you could see
that he had something in his hand.
A small silver fish.
He was stroking it. Placing it in the water
in swimming position.
It floated to the surface and lay on its side.
Once, twice.
The sun shone on the side of the fish
and the boy continued.
Nearby another boy stood with a fishing pole
facing the other way.
He was busy and only looked over once in a while.
The boy continued trying to help the fish
by adjusting it in the water, placing it in motion.
Patiently and deliberately, as if placing the last piece
in a puzzle. As if it only needed a little help, a touch.
Once in a while the fish would actually stir on its own
and then it would slip to the surface as if having died again.
Each time the boy seemed more intent
and repeated his stroking, hovering like a guardian
repeating this ritual of patient affection and concern.

It was a very clear day. The water and the light glittered.
I stayed until I couldn't watch any longer.
Hovering as if to understand.
They were a perfect pair.
The little fish did not know how to go on living.
And the boy did not know how to let it go.

Yvette Neisser Moreno

Born in Portland, Maine, in 1973, she is the author of *Grip*, co-translator of *South Pole/Polo Sur* by María Teresa Ogliastri, and editor of *Difficult Beauty: Selected Poems* by Luis Alberto Ambroggio. With a specialization in the Middle East, she has worked as an international program coordinator, writer, editor, and translator, and has taught at The George Washington University, Catholic University, The Writer's Center, and elsewhere. Raised in California and New Jersey, she lives in Silver Spring, Maryland, with her husband and two children.

The Shape of Faith
    Rosh Hashanah, 1998/5759

All rise—the opening of the ark.
The congregation rustles to its feet,
tassels of talit sway with mumbled prayers
and I ask God, *are you somewhere?*
Sunlight skims the surface of the room,
radiating across the sanctuary,
refracted in eyeglasses and the shine
of polished wood, illumining cylinders
of air. But when I lift my hand
to touch them, the shapes dissipate
into particles, hovering and lit.

The rabbi moves into the congregation
as into a sea of reeds, pausing at each step
as people bend with outstretched prayer books
to touch the Torah in his arms.

Above the ark's wooden doors, brass letters
gleam with their own certainty:
Da lifnei mi atah omed
"Know before whom you stand."

And close to the ceiling
in the circle of a brass lamp,
a wavering flame always burns.
From this, I want to learn
the shape of faith: like a tear
flickering and turning,
shifting colors and keening upward.
Sometimes so transparent,
you can barely discern it's there.

Leslie Neustadt

Born in Poughkeepsie, New York in 1949, she is a former Assistant Attorney General for the state of New York. She took early retirement after being diagnosed with an incurable form of blood cancer. She began writing with women words, a peer writing group. Her poetry and essays have been published in *Akros Review, Awareness Magazine, Cure Magazine, Lies, Boasts and Feelings, Bella Online Literary Review, Poetica Magazine, Prick of the Spindle Journal of Literary Arts, r.kv.ry. Magazine,* and several anthologies, including *Peer Glass –an anthology: writings from Hudson Valley peer groups, Mentor's Bouquet,* and *Uneven Furrows of Our Own Design.* She pursues a wide variety of expressive arts.

The First to Go
Nearly 50% of Jewish children marry outside their faith.

The edges were the first to go.
The fenced yards that defined us,
the cut glass bowls that contained us.
It was only later that the sacred chants,
the velvet scrolls were forgotten.
What once was sweet and thick
as the garnet wine we sanctified,
thinned to a bittersweet brew.
Those of us who are still,
hear faint psalms float to heaven.
Remember dipping braided bread
in wild honey and sage.
We see our ancestors,
shiny, glinting shards,
no longer celebrated by living.

Their exhortation, *dor l' dor*
generation to generation,
a guilty secret tattooed on our arms.
We watch some
born of our seed
walk into the horizon,
welcome the forgetfulness,
the freedom,
the unclouded sky.

Yehoshua November

Born in Miami Beach, Florida in 1979, he has a debut poetry collection, *God's Optimism*, which was named a finalist for the 2010 *Los Angeles Times* Book Prize in Poetry and was selected as the winner of the MSR Poetry Book Award. He teaches writing at Rutgers University and Touro College.

A Jewish Poet

It is hard to be a Jewish poet.
You cannot say things about God
that will offend the disbelievers.
And you always have to remind someone
it wasn't your people who killed their savior.
And Solomon and David are always laughing
over your shoulder
like a father and son ridiculing the unfavored brother.
And you cannot entice people with the sloping
parts of a woman's body
because you must always remain pure.
And every day you have to ask yourself why you're writing
when there is already the one great book.
It is hard to be a Jewish poet.
You cannot say anything about the disbelievers,
which might offend God.

How a Place Becomes Holy

Sometimes a man
will start crying in the middle of the street,
without knowing why or for whom.
It is as though someone else is standing there,
holding his briefcase, wearing his coat.

And from beneath the rust of years,
come to his tongue the words of his childhood:
"I'm sorry," and "God," and "Do not be far from me."

And just as suddenly the tears are gone,
and the man walks back into his life,
and the place where he cried becomes holy.

Baal Teshuvas at the Mikvah

Sometimes you see them
in the dressing area
of the ritual bath,
young bearded men unbuttoning
their white shirts,
slipping out of their black trousers,
until, standing entirely naked,
they are betrayed by the tattoos
of their past life:
a ring of fire climbing up a leg,
an eagle whose feathery wing span
spreads the width of the chest,
or worse, the scripted name of a woman
other than one's wife.

Then, holding only a towel,
they begin, once more, the walk
past the others in the dressing room:
the rabbi they will soon sit before

in Talmud class,
men with the last names
of the first Chasidic families,
almost everyone,
devout since birth.

And with each step,
they curse the poverty
that keeps the dark ink
etched in their skin,

until, finally, they descend the stairs
of the purifying water
and, beneath the translucent liquid,
appear once again
like the next man,

who, in all his days,
has probably never made a sacrifice
as endearing to God.

Idra Novey

Born in Johnstown, Pennsylvania in 1978, she is the author of the 2011 National Poetry Series selection *Exit, Civilian*, which was named a Best Book of 2012 by *Cold Front Magazine* and *The Volta*. Her first book *The Next Country* was a Kinereth Gensler Award winner and a finalist for the ForeWord Book of the Year Award in poetry. Her most recent translations are Viscount Lascano Tegui's novel *On Elegance While Sleeping*, shortlisted for the 2011 Best Translated Book Award, and Clarice Lispector's *The Passion According to G. H.* She's received fellowships from the Poetry Society of America, the National Endowment for the Arts, the PEN Translation Fund, and *Poets & Writers Magazine* and her poems have been featured on NPR's All Things Considered, in *Poetry, The Paris Review, Slate, American Poetry Review, A Public Space,* and elsewhere. She's taught in the MFA Program at Columbia University, at NYU and in the Bard Prison Initiative, and currently teaches in the Creative Writing Program at Princeton University. She lives in Brooklyn, New York with her husband and two sons.

The Other Boat

After a few trips, the first dove
stopped blundering back to Noah
and his couplets of animals.
Then nothing else is known
of that first messenger bird,
if instead of drowning
that first bird found
a great nest of a boat
full of other birds—and all winged
they didn't need anyone

to tell them of the sea.
They could figure forth
as they pleased, observe
all the soaked and sunken things
Noah saw as punishment
now slowly pinking up.

Instead Of

Maybe there's another place for us to leave
and call that leaving wisdom, call it saw-it-once,
call it in-the-absence-of.
                      As our planet does,
we have to revolve around ourselves first
and then a sun. After a sentence behind bars,
the smog outside becomes
                      the fog of Eden,
the forgotten ease of getting lost in Eden.
You can hear it still along the halls of
a penitentiary,
                    the pacing of the guards
and prisoners, of our million nights awake
and thinking, trying to recall where
the Garden might have been.

Lisa Olstein

Born in Boston in 1972, she is the author of *Radio Crackling, Radio Gone*, winner of the Hayden Carruth Award; *Lost Alphabet*, named one of the nine best poetry books of 2009 by *Library Journal*; and *Little Stranger*. She is the recipient of a Pushcart Prize and fellowships from the Massachusetts Cultural Council and Centrum. Her poems have appeared in many literary journals including *The Iowa Review*, *American Letters & Commentary*, *Denver Quarterly*, *Fairy Tale Review*, *Indiana Review*, *notnostrums*, and *Glitterpony*. She is also the lyricist for the rock band Cold Satellite, fronted by Jeffrey Foucault, which has released two albums: *Cold Satellite* and *Cavalcade*. She teaches in the MFA program at the University of Texas-Austin. http://lisaolstein.com

Space Junk

There is a point on every mission
when something must be jettisoned

into the thin black air.
Nothing likes to be abandoned,

no one likes to be compared.
There is a point when the plan

lifts from our control panels
and shimmers while we go ahead

and stare. How long do we
call the plan the plan after it

disappears? There's no such thing
as a few minutes alone. There's no

such thing as making up your mind
when everything is determined:

the rate of our turning, our distance
from the sun. I followed you here

with my naked eye. You've lost
your white glove. It travels now

like a comet burning up the sky.

Man Feeding Bear an Ear of Corn

What we need is an allegory.
What we want is a parable.
What we remember is a face,
a movement of hands like wings.
If god is an absence, what's missing
is blue. If god is a book, its pages
are blue. Doorways appear green.
Night is a small patch in the distance
where everything swirls inviting—
a place, from this distance, you might like
to stay for a while. An arm extends
an ear to an arm extended.
If you have a hand place it over your heart.
This necklace will not be mistaken for its chain.

This is a Test of the Internal Emergency Broadcast System

On her way home from school
your little girl wants spotted mice
from the pet store.

She wants to give them a bath
without losing them in the suds
but they escape their paper bag

and disappear underfoot in the car.
Now your little girl wants
a bright green snake

that won't get lost in the snow.
The red-tipped posts lining
the drive look wounded.

This is not an emergency.
This is winter saying I decapitated
your small glass bird.

Hungry deer step from the woods
on velvet-gloved legs.
This is a test.

Place your elevated heart
rate in this pre-paid self-addressed
steel envelope.

We should all be prepared
to proceed calmly
through the crackling air.

Jacqueline Osherow

Born in Philadelphia in 1956, she received her BA from Harvard-Radcliffe and her Ph.D from Princeton. She is the author of six books of poetry, most recently *Whitethorn*, from LSU Press. She has been awarded fellowships from the John Simon Guggenheim Foundation, the National Endowment for the Arts, the Ingram Merrill Foundation, the Witter Bynner Prize from the American Academy and Institute of Arts and Letters, and a number of prizes from the Poetry Society of America and Pushcart. Her work has appeared in many anthologies and journals, including *The New Yorker, Paris Review, The New Republic, American Poetry Review, Slate, Best American Poetry, Norton Anthology of Jewish-American Literature, The Wadsworth Anthology, Longman Anthology*, and many others. She is Distinguished Professor of English at the University of Utah.

Yom Kippur Sonnet with a Line from Lamentations

Can a person atone for pure bewilderment?
For hyperbole? for being wrong
In a thousand categorical opinions?
For never opening her mouth, except too soon?
For ignoring, all week long, the waning moon
Retreating from its haunt above the local canyons,
Signaling her season to repent,
Then deflecting her repentance with a song?
Because the rest is just too difficult to face –
What we are – I mean – in all its meagerness –
The way we stint on any modicum of kindness –
What we allow ourselves – what we don't learn
How each lapsed, unchanging year resigns us --
Return us to you, Lord, and we'll return.

Hearing News from the Temple Mount in Salt Lake City

You know that conversation
in the elevator in the Catskills:
how one woman says, *Oy,
the food here is so terrible*
and the other *and the portions
are so small*? It's a variant
on Jacob's line to Pharaoh
when he gets to Egypt — *few
and evil have been the days
of my life*. Naturally, he's our
chosen namesake: this Israel
the Torah keeps forgetting and
calling Jacob, as if it doesn't
trust his cleaned-up name... ..

Obviously he's the perfect
guy for us — we're always
willing to take something
over nothing — hence
our lunatic attachment
to that miserable pinpoint
in the desert, where now,
whether it's Ishmael
or Isaac on the altar,
there's an earsplitting
crowd working to drown
out every angel until
Abraham fulfills his sacrifice.

It's none of my diaspora-
befuddled business, but
I'm not in the mood
to celebrate. Call me
thin-skinned, but I can't
get used to the idea that

all these hordes of people
wish me dead. You have
to remember: I'm Jacob's
offspring; I want as many
evil days as I can lay my
hands on … Thank God
I live in Salt Lake City. Who's
going to come looking for me
here? In this calm Zion,
where a bunch of blonde
mishuginers think *they're*
the chosen people of God.
Good luck to them is all
I have to say; let them
get the joy from it that I do.

Ch'vil Schreiben a Poem auf Yiddish

I want to write a poem in Yiddish
and not any poem, but the poem
I am longing to write,
a poem so Yiddish, it would not
be possible to translate,
except from, say, my bubbe's
Galizianer to my zayde's Litvak
and even then it would lose a little something,

though, of course, it's not the sort of poem
that relies on such trivialities, as,
for example, my knowing how to speak
its language—though, who knows?
Maybe I understand it perfectly;
maybe, in Yiddish, things aren't any clearer
than the mumbling of rain on castoff leaves.

Being pure poem, pure Yiddish poem,
my Yiddish poem is above such meditations,

as I, were I fluent in Yiddish,
would be above wasting my time
pouring out my heart in Goyish metaphors.

Even Yiddish doesn't have a word
for the greatness of my Yiddish poem,
a poem so exquisite that if Dante could rise from the dead
he would have to rend his clothes in mourning.
Oh, the drabness of his noisy,
futile little paradise
when it's compared with my Yiddish poem.

His poems? They're everywhere. A dime a dozen.
A photocopier can take them down in no time.
But my Yiddish poem can never be taken down,
not even by a pious scribe
who has fasted an entire year
to be pure enough to write my Yiddish poem,

which exists—doesn't he realize?—
in no realm at all
unless the dead still manage to dream dreams.

It's even a question
whether God Himself
can make out the text of my Yiddish poem.

If He can, He won't be happy.
He'll have to retract everything,
to re-create the universe
without banalities like *firmament* and *light*

but only out of words extracted
from the stingy tongues of strangers,
smuggled out in letters made of camels,

houses, eyes, to deafen
half a continent with argument
and exegesis, each refinement

purified in fire after
fire, singed almost beyond
recognition, but still
not quite consumed, not even
by the heat of my Yiddish poem.

Alan Michael Parker

Born in New York in 1961, he is the author of six collections of poems, including *Long Division*, and two novels, including *Whale Man*. He has been awarded two Pushcart Prizes, the Fineline Prize from the *Mid-American Review*, and the Lucille Medwick Memorial Award from the Poetry Society of America, among other honors. His poems have appeared widely, including in *American Poetry Review*, *Kenyon Review*, *The New Yorker*, *The New Republic*, *The Paris Review*, *Yale Review*, and *Best American Poetry, 2011*. He has been awarded residencies from the MacDowell Colony, VCCA, and the Corporation of Yaddo, and numerous grants, including two from the Arts & Sciences Council. He holds degrees from Washington University and Columbia University, and he teaches at Davidson College, where he is professor of English and director of creative writing, and in the Queens University low-residency MFA program. http://www.amparker.com

Television Psalm

Once a week God
twenty-two minute God
God of a set design

of cliffhanger of mystery guest of newsflash
young God pretty God
made up God remote God

God of sign-in please
God of cancellation
God I will never know

if I die before I
pay what I owe
be merciful be just grant me

a new body
the reek of it and the juice of it
shit and wine

may I walk mid-morning always breezy
on a low mountain may the clouds
pile like pillows on my bed

and always may the pin oaks
guard the gates of my repose
all my feelings in a row.

Dear God who made me act
in whose gaze I am rerun
now I lay me down

in the blue light of your love
and my body is
blue light in the wind

as predicted forthcoming as it is on Earth.
God of the scroll
of what's next soon

are you made of blue light too?
Fill me sieve me sell me
your slave your prophet your profiteer

your made of nothing
your live in the eye of
this my God your ion hurricane.

Hila Ratzabi

Born in Rehovot, Israel in 1981, she has been nominated for a Pushcart Prize, was selected by Adrienne Rich as a recipient of a National Writers Union Poetry Prize, and received an Amy Award. Her poetry has been published in *H_NGM_N, Cortland Review, Coal Hill Review, Southern Poetry Review, Columbia Review, Zeek, Margie,* and *Lumina*. Her chapbook, *The Apparatus of Visible Things*, is published by Finishing Line Press. Her book-length poetry manuscript, *No One Blue*, was a finalist in the To the Lighthouse Poetry Publication Prize. She is the poetry editor of the literary journal *Storyscape* and a former poetry editor of *Lumina*. She holds an MFA in Poetry Writing from Sarah Lawrence College, a BA in English from Barnard College, and a BA in Jewish Philosophy from the Jewish Theological Seminary.

Aubade

I.

I have shown up for morning, a late guest.
Light becomes more light-like, less God-like.
The ordered nonsense of birds gets me through the day.

The body is a day to get through, too.
It's in the way.
The light is full of holes, and nothing gets through.

II.

The sky is nothing
but an emotion
God is having right now.

III.

Where do I take myself from here?
To the Canyon of Thought,
the City of Forgetting?

I would like to place these thoughts
on a subway train
or in the mouth of a gargoyle on a Fifth Avenue building.

They'd sit there like a little group of people, waiting.
They would feel safe in that stone center.
I would let them go.

Hilda Raz

Born in Rochester, New York she now lives in Placitas, New Mexico where she is the series editor for poetry for the University of New Mexico Press, after a long career teaching and editing at the University of Nebraska. She is Luschei Professor and editor of *Prairie Schooner*, Emerita.
http://www.hildaraz.com

Recovery

The fingers of the rain are tapping again.
I send out my heart's drum.
Blood stripe on the feathered tulip dissolves into wet.
All night a low thrumming.

Up, up the two-toned hosta
green from sopped earth.
Along your bruised ribs, cream bells.

Diaspora

The gates were closing and the time was late
in spite of our efforts in the car,
our suitcases packed, our coats tossed off,
goodbyes said, or not to be said

in spite of our efforts in the car
the houses closed, the plants farmed out
goodbyes said, or not to be said
the neighbors told, the little ones in their beds

the houses closed, the plants farmed out
the station doors opening on uniform corridors
the neighbors told, the little ones in their beds
we fanned our faces, opened our books

the station doors opening on uniform corridors
then there was smoke, and damp, and sky
we fanned our faces, opened our books
we shut the windows, began to move

then there was smoke, and damp, and sky
our suitcases packed, our coats tossed off
we shut the windows, began to move
The gates were closing and the time was late

Victoria Redel

Born in New York City in 1959, she is the author of two books of poetry, *Already the World* and *Swoon*, and three books of fiction, most recently the novel *The Border of Truth*. A new collection of poems, *Woman Without Umbrella*, and a story collection, *Make Me Do Things* are also available. Her latest novel, *The Border of Truth*, weaves the situation of refugees and a daughter's awakening to the history and secrets of her father's survival and loss. It was a 2007 Barnes and Noble Discovery Book. The *Los Angeles Times* said: "*The Border of Truth* is such a good novel that it could also be any American's Story." It was adapted for a feature film directed by Kevin Bacon. Her work has been translated into five languages. She is a professor at Sarah Lawrence College. She has received fellowships from the National Endowment for The Arts and the Fine Arts Work Center. She currently serves as vice president of the board of PEN. http://www.victoriaredel.com

Survivor

After textiles my father worked in futures.
He put away the squares of silk and cotton,
taught himself to buy and sell
a thing and never see it.
All abstraction and then the dollar.
Every morning, he bit the lucky silver head.
He kept coins in dresser drawers,
suitcase of currency.

For him the world was a map
of circumstance and the Jew:
bullish and bearish

were only stalling tactics
until a new border guard.

When his wife died a natural death
my father could not cry like one
who entering the beloved temple
sees the arc curtain torn away,
the Torah gone.
My father wept the bewildered tears
of one who had resolved
that even in a crashing market
there was always a future
to be bought back.

Susan Rich

Born in Boston in 1959, Susan Rich makes her home in the Pacific Northwest. She is the author of four collections of poetry: *Cloud Pharmacy*, *The Alchemist's Kitchen*, *Cures Include Travel*, and *The Cartographer's Tongue / Poems of the World*, which won the PEN USA Award for Poetry; all books published by White Pine Press. Her awards include a 4 Culture Award, an Artist Trust Fellowship, a City Artist Award, a Peace Corps Writers Award and a Fulbright Fellowship. Along with Brian Turner and Jared Hawkley, she is editor of *The Strangest of Theatres: Poets Writing Across Borders* published by McSweeney's. Her international work includes editing *The Human* journal published out of Istanbul, Turkey and facilitating workshops at Anam Cara in West Cork, Ireland. She is a professor of English and film studies at Highline Community College and co-founder of Poets on the Coast: A Weekend Writing Retreat for Women.

Different Places to Pray

Everywhere, everywhere she wrote; something is falling –
a ring of keys slips out of her pocket into the ravine below;

nickels and dimes and *to do* lists; duck feathers from a gold pillow.
Everywhere someone is losing a favorite sock or a clock stops

circling the day; everywhere she goes she follows the ghost
of her heart; jettisons everything but the shepherd moon, the
    hopeless cause.

This is the way a life unfolds: decoding messages from profiteroles,
the weight of mature plums in late autumn. She'd prefer a compass

rose, a star chart, text support messages delivered from the net,
even the local pet shop – as long as some god rolls away the gloss

and grime of our gutted days, our global positioning crimes.
Tell me, where do you go to pray – a river valley, a pastry tray?

What to Make of Such Beauty?

> *The attack lasted less than half an hour. Approximately 1,200,000 books and 600 sets of periodicals were destroyed.*
> —Kemal Bakarsic, The Burning of the Sarajevo National Library, 1992

The next day along the streets of Sarajevo
scorched pieces of paper

fluttered like a strange snow.

Peel one scrap from the sky
call it hope and an urgent message

appears ~ for one moment ~

a new form of God pentimento.
Turkish, Hebrew, and Bosnian texts ...

Desire lit in the arabesque of black, besotted alphabets ~

until the warmth of the lines
recede and the magic letters fall like trash ~

fingers chalked in the floating literatures of grief.

Yet, the hardest part, Lejla says
is to not live within such burning,

not breathe in the pages of our indestructible history.

Kim Roberts

Born in Charlotte, North Carolina in 1961, she can trace her heritage on both sides back to the city of Vilnius, now in Lithuania, once considered the world center of Yiddish literature. She is the author of three books of poems, most recently *Animal Magnetism*, and a nonfiction book, *Lip Smack: The History of Spoken Word Poetry in DC*. She is editor of the anthology *Full Moon on K Street: Poems About Washington, DC*, and the online journal *Beltway Poetry Quarterly*. She is the recipient of writer's residencies from 14 artist colonies across the U.S., and poems of hers have been translated into Spanish, Portuguese, German, and Mandarin.
http://www.kimroberts.org

Gefilte

Bottled in translucent jelly,
fished out on a fork,
plated with horseradish.
A corrugated pellicle of parsley,
a coin of carrot. An aspic sheen.

A shudder of grandmothers,
whose new-world-shtetl bathtubs
once swam with fresh fish
before each major holiday,
and who knows how long

that bottle sat, shelf-bound?
The pop, the vacuum-lock pop
of the top of the bottle, the sigh
of air seeping in, in-drawn,
the three types of white fish,

ground and shaped into ovals,
that food I crave, that
bottled bit of history,
and the horseradish so strong
my poor eyes start to burn.

No Jews in Appalachia

When we got to the Hog Scraping Shed
with its huge basin for pouring
boiling water to loosen the bristles
prior to butchering, it was clear:
there were no Jews

among the early settlers
in the Southern Highlands.
The sign explained how they'd tie
those hind trotters, slit the throat
and raise the hog on a pulley.

All the buildings at the museum
were hand-hewn, dovetails joints
and wooden pegs, and beams
pared by hand-axes, all built
before the Civil War

(which the signs insisted on calling
The War Between the States).
After the Hog Shed,
we toured the chapel,
as if more proof were needed.

You put on your thickest Southern accent;
I countered with New York,
my father's accent,
a different kind of beauty,
and soothing to my tongue.

Liz Rosenberg

Born in Glen Cove, New York in 1958, she has published four award-winning books of poems, three novels, two anthologies on Jewish life, edited five prize-winning poetry anthologies and published more than 20 books for young readers. Her work has appeared in *The New Yorker, The Atlantic Monthly, American Poetry Review, The Paris Review, Harper's, The Forward, The New York Times*, and elsewhere. She has won an IRA Choice Award, The Center for the Book Prize, the Paterson Prize, The Atlantic First Prize, and a Kelloggs National Fellowship, among other honors. She is a professor of English, creative writing and Judaic studies at Binghamton University.

Couple on Hospital Elevator

With grime-blackened fingernails
he touches her face with the back of his hand
while she makes that long, slow, secretive swipe
that wipes away weeping.

Flat on her back on the hospital gurney, her hair stubbled short,
the IV bag swaying beside her like a giant tear.
They fix their eyes together on the floor number display

watching it fall, then, still bending toward her,
he follows her into the open lobby,
saying goodbye. And how shall we stand it,
how shall we bear it,
what good can come of this?

I beg you to send them health, Lord,
--or if not health then comfort;
and if not even comfort then brandish a radiance
from your broken sparks

brilliant enough
to make these sorrows possible to bear.

How Quickly, How Early

The fourth grader, his puffy down jacket
blood-red as any cardinal,
flies lightly up the path to school, skidding
when he gets to the open door.
Then, looking strangely
like his father heading in to work,
he stops, shoves back his hood,
braces his shoulders
for the day, and trudges forward.
How quickly, how early such
lessons begin!

Carly Sachs

Born in Detroit in 1979, she was the recipient of the 2011 Stella Kupferberg Memorial Short Story Prize. Her first book of poems, *The Steam Sequence*, won the 2006 Washington Writers' Publishing House book prize. She is the editor of *The Why and Later*, an anthology of poems that women have written about rape and sexual assault. Her poems have appeared in *The Best American Poetry 2004*, *Another Chicago Magazine*, *Nextbook*, *MiPoesis*, *PMS*, *The New Vilna Review*, *The Saint Ann's Review*, and *Present Tense*. She received her MFA from The New School and has taught courses at George Washington University. Currently, she teaches English and yoga at Kent State University.

Shalom
for Justin

The sun rising from the well of your palm,
touch is two moments colliding.

In your hands, the story of the world;
a piano is a poor translator

unless song is warmth
turning ivory into skin

and the distance between any two points
melts into a festival of arrival,

the way hello means peace in the language
of our ancestors.

After the Reading in the Southeast

Anacostia sounds like
a Russian shtetl,
same beginning, same vowel
opening, ana, delicate
lace of streets, handiwork
of dreams as we writers
gather on good hope
road, mid-summer
DC cries Ana, the woman
I could be or the one
I won't be, or the one
I want to be.

Anacostia is my mother's
hand on my forehead
or the slips in her drawer
and trying them on
when she's not there.
Anacostia is lifting
what belongs to you
to your face and closing
your eyes.

What is the bridge between
hearing and understanding,
the difference between sympathy
and empathy? Ana, ana, a, a,
pastel blue, pink and
bone in my hand.

Ira Sadoff

Born in Brooklyn in 1945, he is the author of eight books of poetry, a novel, an *Ira Sadoff Reader* and a critical book on poetics and politics, *History Matters*. His latest collection, *True Faith*, was published by BOA in 2012. He teaches in the MFA program at Drew and Colby College and lives in central Maine.
http://irasadoff.wordpress.com

My Mother's Funeral

The rabbi doesn't say she was sly and peevish,
fragile and voracious, disheveled, voiceless and useless,
at the end of her very long rope. He never sat beside her
like a statue while radio voices called to her from God.
He doesn't say how she mamboed with her broom,
staggered, swayed, and sighed afternoons,
till we came from school to feed her. She never frightened *him*,
or bent to kiss him, sponged him with a fever, never held his hand,
bone-white, bolted doors and shut the blinds. She never sent
roaches in a letter, he never saw her fall down stairs, dead sober.
He never watched her sweep and murmur, he never saw
spider webs she read as signs her life was over, long before
her frightened husband left, long before
they dropped her in a box, before her children turned
shyly from each other, since they never learned to pray.
If I must think of her, if I can spare her moment on the earth,
I'll say she was one of God's small sculptures,
polished to a glaze, one the wind blew off a shelf.

Richard Schiffman

Born in New York City in 1952, he is a writer based in New York, and a former journalist for National Public Radio. He is the author of two biographies: *Mother of All*, and *Sri Ramakrishna, A Prophet For the New Age*. His poems have appeared or are upcoming in *Alaska Quarterly Review*, *Poetry East*, *The North American Review*, *Southern Poetry Review*, *32 Poems*, *Rattle*, *Valparaiso Poetry Review*, *The New York Times*, and many other journals. He is the winner of the Lucidity Poetry Prize and has been twice nominated for a Pushcart. His "Spiritual Poetry Portal" can be found at: http://multiplex.isdna.org/poetry.htm

Balls

Maybe they'll show up on a Sunday like this, when the spring,
which had gone on a chilly sabbatical, saunters back,
the sun a big fat grinning yolk, the breeze a romping puppy,
and everybody and their uncle is out in the park fussing with balls.
What will the little green men think as they watch the local bipeds
toss them and kick them, roll them and spin them, high and low,
fast and slow, whack them with mallets and strike them with bats,
smack them with rackets and snatch them in nets, dunk them
    through hoops
and punch them at holes, push them with sticks and bounce them off
    bricks?
Or just plain lob them endlessly underhand, overhand, back and
    forth,
the bipeds lunging to catch them midair, and the quadrupeds
yelping after them with doggy rapture, even the pinnipeds
spinning the big red ones upon their natty whiskers, as the bipeds
flip them silver fishes. Maybe this ball thing is their religion,
their way of giving thanks for the blue-green ball of earth,

and for the fireball sun. And for their own lives rolled
and tossed and spun through time and space and mind.
Then snagged at the end in a heart-stopping play
in the glove of Heaven's Catcher.

Jason Schneiderman

Born in San Antonio in 1976, he is the author of *Striking Surface*, winner of the Richard Snyder prize from Ashland Poetry Press, and *Sublimation Point*, a Stahlecker Selection from Four Way Books. His poetry and essays have appeared in numerous journals and anthologies, including *American Poetry Review*, *Harvard Review*, *The Best American Poetry*, *Grand Street*, *The Penguin Book of the Sonnet*, *Story Quarterly*, and *Tin House*, among other places. He has received fellowships from Yaddo, The Fine Arts Work Center, and The Bread Loaf Writers' Conference. He was the recipient of the Emily Dickinson Award from the Poetry Society of America in 2004. He currently directs the Writing Center at the Borough of Manhattan Community College.
http://www.jasonschneiderman.net

Probability

And now the world cracks open, like an enormous egg,
but not really, ha ha, nothing really cracks the world open,
not even that meteor that killed the dinosaurs. The world
was fine, still there, even if not quite the world it had been
the day before. Like how Dresden was still there, but not
quite Dresden, or Hiroshima, how it was there, but not quite
Hiroshima. The statistical probability of being a dinosaur
at the moment that the meteor hit is impossible to calculate,
because you would have to know whether any given dinosaur
was as likely to be any other given dinosaur, or whether
any living thing is as likely to be any other living thing,
but no matter what, the chance was tiny. No matter how you do
the math, every single dinosaur was statistically safe from
meteors, but then again, here we are, you and me, as human
and furless as we might have hoped, tiny teeth, opposable
thumbs, and all the birds locked out of our safe, insured
houses.

Lamentation

O dust. O man who is to be dust. O muse
who sings the dust that was man. O dust
that is sung. O broom that sweeps the dust
I sing. O hay that became broom. O stick
that became broom. O broom factory.
O sweeper. O sweeper. O sweeper.

Esther Schor

Born in Tallahassee in 1957, she is working on a second book of poems and on a narrative poem set in Nova Scotia in the 1940s and 1950s. She is also working on a book about Esperanto and the dream of a universal language. Her most recent books include *Strange Nursery* and *Emma Lazarus*.

Alef
For R. B.

Sunday, far north
    the broad air
leafless, farmstands
    hunch at the roadside
boarded, murmur
    a brucha for last fruits –
last pumpkin, last apple,
    last week;
the chill Sabbath
    kept at bay
returns to the schoolroom.
    A moment before learning
what do we remember?
    lamed, a lamp
mem, a mouth
    taf; a table, a tack
as though all letters
    bloomed into things
as though God were wandering
    the vineyard, blessing
the heavy vines. But God's become
    forgetful, we've all noticed

the change; frost cracks
    the folding husks
binds the soil
    where we planted
marigolds; my daughter paints
    in crimson streaks
alef, akimbo, unimaged:
    it says nothing
because the sound it says is
    invisible

Philip Schultz

Born in Rochester in 1945, he is an American poet and the founder/director of The Writers Studio, a private school for fiction and poetry writing based in New York City. He is the author of several collections of poetry, including his most recent, *Failure*, co-winner of the 2008 Pulitzer Prize in Poetry, *Living in the Past*, and *The Holy Worm of Praise*, all published by Harcourt. He is also the author of *Deep Within the Ravine*, *Like Wings* and the poetry chapbook, *My Guardian Angel Stein*. He lives in East Hampton, New York with his wife, sculptor Monica Banks, and their two sons.

I Remember
for Yehuda Amichai

I remember walking you home so you could walk me home
so I could walk you halfway back, until, finally,
you walked one block to finish a last story like a blessing.

I remember our wandering around the Circus Maximus
of Times Square to Mozart, you proved, beating time
on my back, your hand in the crowd conducting ecstasy.

I remember the warm yogurt of the Dead Sea,
wiggling our toes and balancing the sun on our noses
like comedian seals, God, for once, speechless.

I remember the Jerusalem you showed me like a wound,
every tree, street, and shadowed doorway.
I remember the stars burning in the night like graves.

I remember our driving eight hundred miles
to move my mother into a nursing home, your kissing
her hand like a soldier saluting an act of courage.

I remember our silence at the Western Wall,
our prayers hovering in the air like hummingbirds.
I remember your smiling as if everything had been forgiven.

I remember our singing Vallejo, Transtromer, Szymborska,
in a classroom, the joy in your hooded eyes,
the cancer scraping your blood like a scythe.

I remember your drifting off in cafes like an astronaut
turning in space, attached only by an umbilicus of faith,
the light in your eyes moving farther and farther away.

The Children's Memorial at Yad Vashern
for Hana Amichai

Inside a domed room photos of children's faces
turn in a candlelit dark as recorded voices
recite their names, ages and nationality.
"Ah, such beautiful faces," a woman sighs.
Yes, but faces without prestige
of the future or the tolerance of the past.
Not one asks: Why is this happening to me?
They stare at the camera as if it were a commandment:
thou shall not bear false witness...

Why would anyone want to take their photo,
remember what they no longer looked like?
There's no delusion in their eyes,
no recognition or longing, only
the flames of hours without minutes,
hunger without appetite.

They understand they are no longer children,
that death is redundant, and mundane.
Expected, like a long-awaited guest
who arrives bearing the gift
of greater anticipation. Their eyes

are heavy—fear perhaps,
or the unforgiving weight
of knowledge.

Did they understand why they were so hated?
Wonder why they were Jews?

Did God hear their prayers and write
something in one of his glistening books?

Were they of too little consequence?
What did they think of God, finally?

Dante cannot help us.
Imagination is the first child in line.
They cannot help us.
It is wrong to ask them.
Philosophy cannot help us,
nor wisdom, or time.
Or memory.

We look at their faces and their faces look at us.
They know we are pious.
They know we grieve.
But they also know we will soon leave.
We are not their mothers and fathers,
who also could not save them.

Why

is this man sitting here weeping
in this swanky restaurant
on his 61st birthday, because
his fear grows stronger each year,
because he's still the boy running
all out to first base, believing
getting there means everything,
because of the spiders climbing

the sycamore outside his house
this morning, the elegance of
a civilization free of delusion,
because of the boyish faces
of the five dead soldiers on TV,
the stoic curiosity in their eyes,
their belief in the righteousness
of sacrifice, because innocence
is the darkest place in the universe,
because of the Iraqis on their hands
and knees, looking for a bloody button,
a bitten fingernail, evidence of
their stolen significance, because
of the primitive architecture
of his dreams, the brutal egoism
of his ignorance, because he believes
in deliverance, the purity of sorrow,
the sanctity of truth, because of
the original human faces of his wife
and two boys smiling at him across
this glittering table, because of
their passion for commemoration,
their certainty that goodness continues,
because of the spiders clinging to
the elegance of each moment, because
getting there still means everything?

Howard Schwartz

Born in St. Louis, Missouri in 1945, he is the author of four books of poems: *Vessels, Gathering the Sparks, Sleepwalking Beneath the Stars,* and *Breathing in the Dark.* He is also the co-editor of *Voices Within the Ark: the Modern Jewish Poets.* His other books include *Tree of Souls: The Mythology of Judaism,* which won the National Jewish Book Award in 2005, and *Leaves from the Garden of Eden: One Hundred Classic Jewish Tales,* published in 2008. His new book, *The Library of Dreams: New and Selected 1965-2013,* is forthcoming. http://www.howardschwartz.com

Signs of the Lost Tribe

One day
I found the first sign:
old boxes stacked in the attic
in a room I had never entered.
After that
I found the signs everywhere:
in every drawer I opened,
on every doorpost I passed,
when I lay down
and when I rose up.

Somehow
one of the ten lost tribes
had wandered
out of the desert,
and all of them were living
in my house.

Since then
I have become accustomed

to their ways.
Of course, I never acknowledge
their presence.
Who knows
what they would do
if their secret were known?

They have traveled in exile
ever since they were born,
following the path of the exodus
wherever it leads them.

Somehow, they still fulfill
the rituals
carved out of so many years
of wandering:
blessing the moon,
counting the stars,
casting their sins in the water.

During the day
they search everywhere
for the land that has been lost.
At night, they hide
from the unsuspecting
in closets filled with invisible families,
in drawers crowded with sorrows,
on shelves full of their sad
songs.

They even inhabit
my dreams.
There,
above all,
they are at home.

Breathing in the Dark
    for Ava

So many months breathing in the dark—
the scent of underground springs
sustains you,
a hidden moon beckons you
to grow ripe.

While you sleep,
an angel whispers the secrets of creation,
showing you
every branch of the tree of life.
Someday
you will dimly recall
all that was revealed,
roots
and branches
and breath.

You wake,
a lilac
waiting for the wind,
a sensual stone,
a leaf
thirsty for a kiss.
From now on
you will wake with this thirst
every morning
and drink in
everything
until the crickets rub their wings together,
singing.

In That Country

> *You will find no other lands.*
> C. P. Cavafy

In that country
there are no gates
to enter or exit.
No passports are required.
No visas to be stamped.
By the time you get there
it's already too late
to turn back.

In that country
there is no waiting for rooms,
nor any rooms for waiting.
Despite all your plans,
no one comes to welcome you.
The phones are all silent.
The traffic has come to a halt.

There are no maps to read,
no landmarks to guide you,
no signposts,
no stations on the way.
Besides, all the roads
lead to the same place.

In that country
all the histories remain unwritten,
all the books are blank.
Not even the cycle of the seasons
is known,
or how long you must stay
before you can set out
for somewhere else.

Ruth L. Schwartz

Born in Geneva, New York in 1962, she has published five books of poems: *Miraculum, Dear Good Naked Morning, Edgewater, Singular Bodies,* and *Accordion Breathing and Dancing.* Ruth has won over a dozen national awards and grants for her work, including the National Poetry Series, the Associated Writing Programs poetry book competition, and fellowships from the NEA, the Ohio Arts Council, and the Astraea Foundation. She is also the author of a spiritual guide book, *Soul on Earth: A Guide to Living & Loving Your Human Life* and a memoir, *Death in Reverse,* and often publishes creative nonfiction in *The Sun.* In addition to her work as a core faculty member in Ashland University's low-residency MFA program, Ruth is a transformational coach and healer who maintains a private practice and teaches retreats nationwide. Her website is: www.EvolutionarySupport.com

Music for Guitar and Stone

In music I can love the small failures,
the ones which show how difficult it is:
the young guitarist's fingers slipping,
for an instant, from their climb of chords.
He sits alone on the stage, bright light,
one leg wedged up on a step, his raised knee
round and tender, and the notes like birds
from a vanishing flock, each one more exquisite and lonely;
the fingers part of the hand, yet separate from the hand,
each living muscle married to the whole.
In life the failures feel like they'll kill me,
or you will, or we'll kill each other;
it's so hard to feel the music
moving through us, the larger patterns

of river and mountain, where damage is not separate
from creation, transformation;
where every mistake we make can wash
smooth and clean as stones in water,
then land on shore, then be thrown in again.
I want to sleep, like a stone, for a thousand years.
I want to wake with creatures traced smooth on my skin.
I want to forget I loved you and failed you
as you failed and loved me too, in the lengthy, painful
evolution of our kind; I want to sleep
for a thousand years, then wake up in some other world
where failure is part of the music, and seen
to make it more beautiful; where the fingers
forgive each other; where we can sit naked again
at the window, watch the notes fly by like birds
who have finally found their way home.

Peter Serchuk

Born in New York City in 1952, his poems have appeared in a variety of journals, including *Boulevard, Poetry, Denver Quarterly, North American Review, Texas Review, South Carolina Review, New Letters,* and others. Additionally, a number of his poems have been anthologized, most recently in *Against Agamemnon: War Poetry* and *The Best American Erotic Poems 1800 to the Present*. His poetry collections include *Waiting for Poppa at the Smithtown Diner* and *All That Remains*.
http://peterserchuk.com

The Hungry Jew
Yankee Stadium, 1965

Yom Kippur is how you separate
the Jews from the jews.
Not Chanukah or Purim with their latkes
and laughter, not Shavuo or Tu B'Shevat...
God himself can't remember the months.
And Rosh Hashana, holy as it is,
trumpets one more circle, a clean step forward,
as unJewish an idea as happiness itself.

But Yom Kippur, when we feast
on the same dust left to Moses above Canaan,
on the same dust that bore witness to
Hank Greenberg's giant shoes, that's when
we tell Him that we, the chosen ones, are here
to earn his blessings, to beg his forgiveness
no matter whose game or rules.
That's why today, World Series be damned,
that's handsome Don Drysdale on the mound
and not the hungry Jew, Sandy Koufax.

Einstein in California

Though his favorite playground
sat between his ears,
he loved the fat, easy days
of a California summer.
Swinging in a hammock in Alta Dena,
he couldn't help but measure
the universe that had him trading
licks at the Bowl with Rodsinski
and belly laughs with Chaplin.
Flattered and feted, he calculated
the improbability of his fame,
the absurdity of the FBI in suits and ties
as they trailed him on the beach.
Later, watching the red ball of August
wade into Santa Monica Bay,
he surveyed the mass of grief
descending, his own escape,
and wondered at the fields of grace
which lace the galaxy.
Some miracles defy all understanding,
he thought. *And happiness*
demands no genius at all.

Patty Seyburn

Born in Detroit in 1962, she has published three volumes of poetry. Her third book, *Hilarity*, won the Green Rose Prize given by New Issues Press. Her two previous books of poems are *Mechanical Cluster* and *Diasporadic* which won the 1997 Marianne Moore Poetry Prize and the American Library Association's Notable Book Award for 2000. Her poems have appeared in numerous journals, including *The Paris Review, Poetry, New England Review, Field, Slate, Crazyhorse, Cutbank, Quarterly West, Bellingham Review, Boston Review, Cimarron Review, Third Coast,* and *Western Humanities Review*. She recently won a 2011 Pushcart Prize for her poem, "The Case for Free Will," published in *Arroyo Literary Review*. She earned a BS and an MS in Journalism from Northwestern University, an MFA in Poetry from University of California, Irvine, and a Ph.D in Poetry and Literature from the University of Houston. She is an associate professor at California State University, Long Beach. She is co-editor of *POOL: A Journal of Poetry*:
http://www.poolpoetry.com

Beruryah, Deciding
    2nd Century, C. E.

I.

Here is a chair, here is a rope with a looped end coiled
as though to hook an answer to some midrashic melee

concerning the value—not in coin or possession—of life,
once arrogance (slender, poised) has spread its venom,

unseated restraint. Eve thought she could handle
all the knowing, keep its desire in check. So did I,

engaging the shul-boys—and men—in argument, peppery
debate ornate with analogy, each point honed as a needle

darning the fabric of law, material rent and sewn so often
that the body is all seams, meetings where text is tested

against the law's undroppable stitch. I have been tested
and not held up so well. My husband, Rabbi Meir, convinced

of women's mercurial nature, sent a student to seduce me,
proving I carry my gender's flaw. I could have saved him

the trouble. I saw a boy and bisected myself: body
and *shechinah*, material and spirit; I left the good girl

in the kitchen kneading, and searched for stories
to serve—poor substitutions, I know—as explanation.

II.

My mother taught me how to tell a person what he
can hear: in verse, song, parable, anecdote, riddle,

and I often told my husband stories to coax him
toward conclusions. My sons both died on a Sabbath,

and I couldn't tell him, couldn't let death infect the day
of rest. He asked, *Where are my sons?* and I turned our loss

into query: *A stranger lent me valuables and wants them back.
Must I return them? Of course,* my husband affirmed, and I

showed him: *The Lord giveth, the Lord…*you know the rest.
My sons, my sons… I felt myself drowning in *halachah*,

our laws, and dreamed myself awash in text, imprinted
on hands, and mouth, bracelets of letters, interpretive limbs,

questions covering breasts and back… When the boy
appeared at my door, I tore myself from the page, tearing

the page itself, curious how it would feel to err by intent.
I am cursed with awareness: we favor the simple son

over the wicked; ignorance pales in the flushed light
of conscious decision. Did I boast myself immune to sin?

III.

I should know what lurks behind songs of seduction,
a script's façade—Jews build furnished rooms of meaning

into our words—still so light they can be carried on
our backs, no need (yes, desire?) for a temple to house

our scrolls. As I took the boy into my hands, so will I
embrace my own punishment: lithe from the rope's grip,

cleansed of choice. Will I be a symbol for what fails
when a woman—a scholar—purges dust from the texts?

I told my husband to pray for the death of a sin,
not the death of a sinner. Will he pray for me, for my pride,

or for his own soul, that which drove him to act as God
commanding the angel to wrestle Jacob, testing his strength?

Had Jacob failed, would the angel have sung hosannas,
or skulked back to God? And God, in His house on high—

whose side was He on? No punishment fits its crime. One apple:
expulsion, pain, the constant ledge of extinction. I say to Eve:

let the sin dissolve into the valence of day and dusk;
let night's calming conscience still the sinner of flux.

Alan Shapiro

Born in Boston in 1952, he is a member of the American Academy of Arts and Sciences, and has published ten books of poems: *After the Digging*, *The Courtesy*, *Happy Hour* which won the 1987 William Carlos Williams Award from the Poetry Society of America and was a finalist for the National Book Critics Circle Award, *Covenant*, *Mixed Company*, winner of the *Los Angeles Times* Book Award in poetry, *The Dead Alive and Busy*, winner of the 2001 Kingsley Tufts Award from Claremont Graduate University, *Song and Dance*, *Tantalus in Love*, *Old War*; his most recent book, *Night of the Republic*, was nominated for a national Book Award. Shapiro is the author of three books of prose, including *The Last Happy Occasion*, which was a finalist for the National Book Critics Circle Award in autobiography in 1997, and *Vigil*, a memoir about his sister's death from breast cancer. His novel, *Broadway Baby*, was published by Alonguin Books in 2012. He has published a translation of *The Oresteia* by Aeschylus and *The Trojan Women* by Euripides. The William R. Kenan, Jr. Distinguished Professor at the University of North Carolina, Shapiro has also taught in the MFA Creative Writing program at UNC, Greensboro, Warren Wilson, and at Northwestern University.

Lethe

You called me to come see the bees. Come out of the house
you called once, in a bad time, when we were lost to each other,
blurred by habitual regard, disgruntled and aloof
though not from injuries, but from a hoarded sense
of being injured, precious so long as vague, vague
        so long as silent.

By the marigolds you planted they were all hovering,
hundreds of bees, it seemed, like bright flecks of lavish

blossoms they were drawn to, each long stalk tipping over
under the pressure as they clung together, crowded and swarmed
the way Virgil says the souls do by the waters
                in Elysium:

even there among the blessed groves, the lush green
of bodiless pleasure, weightless now, unrestricted,
free, they swarm to drink oblivion and again put on
the body's weight. I leaned down close to look, to see
what you saw, and as I did, unconsciously you rested
                one hand on my shoulder,

in an old way, dormant for how long? Time, unresting time,
beautiful and perverse, how suddenly it could lift us
clear of our own shade to a luminous attention
it just as suddenly extinguished, as the bees moved on,
the shade, now, darker for that brief respite. *Poor souls*, Aeneas asks,
                how can they crave our daylight so?

Mezuzah

A small case containing a parchment scroll on which a portion of Deuteronomy is written, attesting to God's everlasting love. It is said whoever breaks open the Mezuzah and removes the sacred scroll will incur God's everlasting retribution.

Though unable to imagine
how harm could fit in there,
in that tiny case,
I thought I knew enough
to stay afraid.
                But once,
moving through the quiet house,
I thought, if I can't hear
my own steps, how can God?
And in the laundry room,
by the dryer humming out its heat,
the thick air,

itself, a kind of linen
covering me, unseen,
unnoticed, I knelt down,
and all I was supposed to fear
I crushed
        with my mother's iron.
The little parchment, speckled
with marks too small to read,
fell out ...
        and nothing happened:
only the washer jerked
into its spin, and made me wait
a little longer
for my blood to turn to salt,
for my hands to wither,
        for pain.
But nothing happened.
        And later,
playing with my friends, I knew
there was no mark of Cain
upon my forehead, no
lightning come to split me
like a tree.
        Only something else,
from then on,
wouldn't go away, kept me
up late at night, damaging
my prayers, til even they no longer tamed
the dark
world of my room:
I knew God's wrath, all right,
His retribution coiled,
forever,
in my questioning.

How

In the bedroom of the afterlife a phone is ringing
On a bedside table beside a bed whose sheet
Is smooth as steel, the crypt-cold pillow unindented,
And how the absence of a blanket on the hard bed's
White sheet on which the pillow rests reveals
The cold's irrelevance, how nothing heavier
Has ever lay down on it than the blanket
That isn't there, the ringing of the phone that never stops,
And how it rings and rings is how the living call,
And how the dead reply is how it goes on ringing.

Maureen A. Sherbondy

Born in Metuchen, New Jersey in 1964, she has poems appearing in *Zeek, European Judaism, Calyx,* and other journals. Her books include *After the Fairy Tale, Praying at Coffee Shops, Weary Blues, Scar Girl, The Year of Dead Fathers,* and *Eulogy for an Imperfect Man.* She lives in Raleigh, North Carolina.

Tashlich

I cut the fish,
lift fleshy pink
sliver to my lips.

How many sins
have you swallowed
dead salmon.

Jews toss
transgressions
into the water.

> Breadcrumbs of infidelity
> Pebbles of lies
> Pocket dust of indifference

I chew and swallow
hope my body
stays free

from what
I have
eaten.

How do we live
with our sins
that return;

a small pebble
caught in the back
of our throat.

David Shevin

His books include *Three Miles from Lucky*, *Needles and Needs*, and *The Discover of Fire*, which won the Ohioana Book Award for poetry. He is the recipient of fellowships from both the National Endowment for the Arts and the Ohio Arts Council. Long active on issues in the peace and civil rights communities, he received the Peacemaker Award from Tiffin's Martin Luther King Committee, and the Cultural Diversity Education Award from the Black Heritage Library Association. One can find his books at Bottom Dog Press, where the estate and press will donate half the profits from book sales of David's books to the ACLU.

Tiger Lilies

They come from everywhere, like summer radio.
In an instant, the north tier's orange harvest
embraces the roadsides and yards and garage boundaries:

each blossom a six pointed star of thanksgiving
each petal a perfect and deep tureen, a breast
rich with perfume. Seven stamens in six petals

in each of this cluster of five burgeoning psalms.
I came to this place with my own stupid music,
a private recycling of novelty tunes no one else can stand

least of all young people. That's a privilege
of youth, to own all your own stupid music. But now
all the new birth belongs in this Eden, this Tiger's

paradise, and the sound is the color of fruit flesh
and flower. What are they thinking? Knowing that
they can get by on their looks, and yet they are so many,

so many, so many? They must sense and smell each other.
Dogs can, and these are more brilliant than dogs are.
They must HEAR each other in such coordination.

They must know something, to make such statement:
"Shut off your stupid music a while. There's LIFE
going on and you'll never control it, you can't even know it

and it's richer than Gates and more orange than sex
and it's louder than God and it's sweeter than sweeter than
sweeter than sweeter than sweeter than sweeter than sweet.

The Call

I look suddenly to the telephone
As though it might ring.
Some nights there is a soft
Violet hue to the storming sky.

The color you might decorate
The inside of your coffins with.
I pick up the receiver. the hum
Is also soft, deeper than I remember.

This is Irene, talking to me
In the silences the dead use
As vocabulary. How does she hear
When I gag and stutter? Where

Do the black bones connect,
Send their nerves? Oh it is good
To hear you, I Lie. Why didn't
You call when you breathed

And had the job at the health spa?
And she says I'm surprised
You recognized my voice.
Or something like that.

It's hard to tell. it's really
A hum, or lightning on a pole.
Everything metal in the room
Demands its own light. The scissors.

The needle. The paper clip.
They burn like baby stars.
The people partying upstairs
Yell, "Would you turn down those lights?"

Jason Shinder

Born in Brooklyn in 1955, he died in 2008 in Manhattan after a battle with lymphoma and leukemia. He was the author of three collections of poetry: the posthumously published *Stupid Hope*, *Among Women*, and *Every Room We Ever Slept In*, a New York Public Library Notable Book. In a review of *Among Women*, poet Carol Muske-Dukes observed, "I don't know of any male poet that approximates the honest terror and desire, the sense of shock that runs through these poems. The poems in *Among Women* are so fixed in a merciless surgical light and yet they're so tender and alive with emotion." He edited ten anthologies, including *The Poem That Changed America: "Howl" Fifty Years Later*, *Tales from the Couch: Writers on Talk Therapy*, and *Divided Light: Father and Son Poems*.

At Sunset

Your death must be loved this much.

You have to know the grief—now.
Standing by the water's edge,

looking down at the wave

touching you. You have to lie,
stiff, arms folded, on a heap of earth

and see how far the darkness

will take you. I mean it, this, now—
before the ghost the cold leaves

in your breath, rises;

before the toes are put together
inside the shoes. There it is—the goddamn

orange-going-into-rose descending

circle of beauty and time.
You have nothing to be sad about.

Alone for the Fifth Day

When I look at the ocean for a long time, the blue

and restless driven waves, I keep looking, I keep looking,
I keep looking at the waves swaying in the wind

like a metronome, wired for the sound of a sleeping heart,

and I keep looking with the silence of the sun
on the windowpane, and I keep looking and do not stop

looking deeper into waves as if into the middle

of a woman's body, where the soul and spirit
have no human bonds, and I begin never to turn away

from looking though I am frightened but keep looking

beyond what I know until I can hardly think or breathe
because I have arrived, with the need to be me disappearing

into the beautiful waves, reflecting no one, nothing, no one.

Jane Shore

Her poetry has garnered accolades from critics and prestigious awards in her field. She is the author of five books of poems: *Eye Level*, winner of the 1977 Juniper Prize; *The Minute Hand*, awarded the 1986 Lamont Prize; *Music Minus One*, a finalist for the 1996 National Book Critic Circle Award; *Happy Family*; and *A Yes-or-No Answer*, winner of the 2010 Poets' Prize. Her latest book is *That Said: New and Selected*.

Last Words

> *Once the patient stops drinking liquids, he's got*
> *up to 14 days to live. If he takes even a sip*
> *of water, you reset the clock.*

Eleven days without a drop. The rabbi
made his rounds. They stopped her
IV and her oxygen. I asked them
to please turn off the TV's live feed
to the empty hospital chapel, lens
focused on the altar and crucifix—
it seemed like the wrong God watching
over her, up there, near the ceiling.
And because hearing is the last
sense to go, the nice doctor spoke
to me in a separate room. He said
it's time to say good-bye. Next day,
he returned her to her nursing home
to die. Her nurses said just talk
to her; let her hear a familiar voice.
I jabbered to the body in the bed.
I kept repeating myself, as I'd done

on visits before, as if mirroring
her dementia. I rubbed her hand,
black as charcoal from the needles.
I talked the way a coach spurs on
a losing team. Suddenly she opened
her eyes, smiled her famous smile,
she *knew* me, and for the first time
in a year of babbling, she spoke
my name, then, in her clearest voice
said, "I love you. You look beautiful.
This is wonderful." I urged her
to sip water through a straw. Then
two cold cans of cranberry juice,
she was that thirsty. Her fingertips
pinked up like a newborn's.
I wanted the nurses to acknowledge
my miracle, to witness my devotion
although I'd been absent all spring.
They reset the clock, resumed her oxygen.
I was like God, I'd revived her. Now
I'd have to keep talking to keep her alive.

A Yes-or-No Answer

Have you read The Story of O?
Will Buffalo sink under all that snow?
Do you double-dip your Oreo?
Please answer the question yes or no.

The surgery—was it touch-and-go?
Does a corpse's hair continue to grow?
Remember when we were simpatico?
Answer my question: yes or no.

Do you want another cup of joe?
If I touch you, is it apropos?

Are you certain that you're hetero?
Is your answer yes or no?

Did you lie to me, like Pinocchio?
Was forbidden fruit the cause of woe?
Did you ever sleep with that so-and-so?
Just answer the question: yes or no.

Did you nail her under the mistletoe?
Will you spare me the details, blow by blow?
Did she sing sweeter than a vireo?
I need an answer. Yes or no?

Are we still a dog-and-pony show?
Shall we change partners and do-si-do?
Are you planning on the old heave-ho?
Check an answer: Yes o No o.

Was something blue in my trousseau?
Do you take this man, this woman? Oh,
but that was very long ago.
Did we say yes? Did we say no?

For better or for worse? Ergo,
shall we play it over, in slow mo?
Do you love me? Do you know?
Maybe yes. Maybe no.

Joan I. Siegel

Born in New York City in 1946, she is the author of *Light at Point Reyes* and *Hyacinth for the Soul* and co-author of *Peach Girl: Poems for a Chinese Daughter*. She is the recipient of both the *New Letters* Award and the Anna Davidson Rosenberg Prize. Her work is widely published in journals and periodicals including *The American Scholar*, *The Atlantic Monthly*, *Prairie Schooner*, *The Gettysburg Review*, *Raritan*, *Carolina Quarterly*, *Commonweal*, and *Hawaii Pacific Review*, among numerous other publications, and in a variety of anthologies.

Hyacinth for the Soul

Bake two loaves of bread, my mother used to say.
Give one away and plant a hyacinth for the soul.
I never understood and she did not explain.
It was one of those sayings from the old country.

Give one away and plant a hyacinth for the soul
as if the soul would not prefer two loaves of bread.
It was one of those sayings from the old country
that my Polish grandmother passed on to her daughters.

As if the soul would not prefer two loaves of bread
hungry and alone in its room beneath the heart
that my Polish grandmother passed on to her daughters:
Oh, soul who are you? What do you know?

Hungry and alone in my room beneath the heart,
I sit out the bruised hours wondering,
Oh, soul who are you? What do you know?
until a poem rises through the dead leaves. Flowers.

I sit out the bruised hours wondering
who are the faces in the photographs
until words rise through the dry leaves. Flower.
I kneel in the dirt, plant hyacinths for my mother.

Who are the faces in the photographs?
I never understood and she did not explain.
So I kneel in the dirt, plant hyacinths for my mother,
bake two loaves of bread as she used to say.

M. E. Silverman

Born in New Jersey in 1970, he spent most of his life in the heart of Louisiana. His chapbook, *The Breath Before Birds Fly*, is available. He is editor and founder of *Blue Lyra Review*. His work has appeared in over 70 journals, including *Crab Orchard Review*, *Chicago Quarterly Review*, *Hawai'i Pacific Review*, *Many Mountains Moving*, *The Southern Poetry Anthology*, *The Los Angeles Review*, *Mizmor L'David Anthology: The Shoah*, *Cloudbank*, *The Broad River Review*, *Pacific Review*, *Because I Said So Anthology*, *Sugar House Review*, and other magazines. He was a finalist for the 2008 New Letters Poetry Award, the 2008 DeNovo Contest, and the 2009 *Naugatuck River Review* Contest. Find more at: http://mesilverman.com

The Last Jew
    for Zablon Simintov, the last Jew of Afghanistan

Sometimes we all feel like the last,
a single stick in a rushing river.
Honestly, who has not felt
hairs rise on the base of their neck
when hands cup to other ears
full of distressing whispers? Listen:

today you are the Last Jew.

You could be in Calcutta or Krakow,
any place given to time
for those *olim* who made *aliyah*.
"Next year in Jerusalem"
they said dutifully
until they did.

Today you are the Last

Jew, the chosen carpet dealer
in the heart of Kabul
where Hebrew letters breathe
like morning birds,
where echoes sink in surrounding streets,
unswept rooms and broken glass,
an eerie emptiness,
a staleness under cracked fans
and dusty cupboards
of books, hundreds
of years old, where God
grumbles to you and you alone.

Every Friday night,
the missing make a slight noise
that sounds like leaves,
sounds like sand,
like wings passing
by, flutters in the sky.

Do you hoist the Torah
above your shoulders, bear it
around the sanctuary for ghosts
to touch it with their *tallises*?
On the Sabbath, do you kiss
the book? Recite the prayers?
Who do you preach to? Who
in your synagogue is teaching?

"I don't know why I'm still
living here." To anyone
who cares, you say
the reason you stay, avoid
seeing your wife for over a decade
and your two Zionist children
is "God's will," but when
Moses confronted the pharaoh

or when Abraham left his home in Ur,
God never instructed them to become
like locust living off what the land offers,
to abandon their family.

So you watch, you wait—
we wonder. Today

you are the Last Jew.

The Last Jew (ii)

    will be born sometime
        after
        you read this,

    with matzah colored skin
        and Talmudic
        eyes,

    with the breath
        of a lost language
        that speaks
            to salt and ash,

    begins
        with *baruch,*
        beginning of a prayer,
            which most ignore

    like the bearded veteran
        who holds a sign
        which could be a board
            from the ark

    on the corner
        of Main
        and 10th.
            For a few,

                    it will feel familiar
                                like the moment
                                right before

                a sneeze
                                and the bless
    you, a fraction
    of a second

        where you know
                            what will come next,
                            and then
                            it is
                            gone.

Bubbie's Kitchen Secret

    Hell's Kitchen, New York City 1983

We cooked in her kitchen,
a small square room
with a large double sink.
The refrigerator zapped
its electric ache
and like an old noir film,
the lights flickered in response.

For herbs, she had me climb
onto the counter and open
the one window to reach
the basil, the thyme, the sunflowers
potted on the fire escape,
a hazardous garden
the whole building used.

Two or three steps were lined
with mason jars full of cucumbers,
for pickles crisp from sunlight.

On this particular Sabbath,
I did what I always did,
helped her make the kugel,
a pudding made of noodles and eggs
with a dash of her secret:
the caramel color from sugar burnt:
not too little, not too much.

We were finishing up
when we smelled the cigar smoke
and heard heavy boots
pounding down the fire escape.

Then glass breaking,
a curse, *that* curse,
quick and sharp
in gun-shot German.

Bubbie screamed. Scared,
I ducked under the table.
She whispered one word
before fainting.
My gold-chained *chai*
fell fast, a train bell's echo.

Ritual for Learning a History

Father loves matzah balls more than me,
more than anyone. He doesn't pause for them
to cool, a child with his prize.

I wait for the four glasses of wine,
the bitter herbs, the tightening
of his eyes and cheeks,

his shoulders and arms,
as he tells the same stories
every year: how he sacrificed

so much to be a Dad
after his own deserted them
with the rabbi's most buxom daughter,

how he spent his monthly ten-cent treat
on sci-fi books, the buses it took to get
out of Sheepshead Bay,

how his mother threw away issue one
of Action, now worth a quarter of a million,
because he once asked where his Dad had gone,

how he shouted out the open door
about her refusal to learn to drive,
to move from the tired bricks of Brooklyn,

to breach her routine that lasted for forty years,
the hot months he peddled down Fifth like a commandment
and up First delivering silk for tips.

Hal Sirowitz

Born in New York City in 1949, he is the former Poet Laureate of Queens, New York. His first collection of poetry, *Mother Said*, was translated into nine languages, including Hebrew. He is the author of three other books of poetry and one forthcoming from Backwaters Press in Nebraska. His poems were put to music by the composer Alla Borzova and were awarded a Susan Rose Recording Grant from the National Jewish Foundation.

No Return

> *"(Prayer is) an appeal which must never be answered; if it is, it ceases to be prayer and becomes correspondence."*
> Oscar Wilde

You should be thanking your
lucky stars that God doesn't
answer your prayers, father said.
Otherwise, you'd have to write
Him a thank you letter for responding.
Then your friends will say,
'I've heard God answers you.
Could you put in a good word
for us, too.' And before you know it,
you'll have to pray
for the whole junior high
and the younger classes, too.
This way, if He doesn't answer,
you could blame it on the acoustics in your room.

Who Are We Fooling?

We end every prayer
in temple, father said,
with the same ending,
'Amen,' which proves
that man may have
the last word but God
is still the master of silence.

Judith Skillman

Born in 1954, Skillman's new collections are *Broken Lines – The Art & Craft of Poetry* (Lummox Press, 2013), and *The Phoenix – New and Selected Poems 2007–2013* (Dream Horse Press). Her poems have appeared in *Poetry, Prairie Schooner, FIELD,* and elsewhere. She is the recipient of grants from the Academy of American Poets, the Washington State Arts Commission, the Centrum Foundation, and the King County Arts Commission.
Visit www.judithskillman.com

The Theory of Space Travel
for Tom

First you must long to be both
things: the sleep and the sleeper,
the traveler and the destination,

the lover and the loved.
We have talked of a room
traveling at the speed of light

while elsewhere in this house
our children grow up, age, and die.
And all of it has happened

just as you said it would,
without our knowing. that's why you
can rest easy, your body massed on the futon,

sleeping equally in the years or single moment
we have left.
the candle we lit before our lovemaking

lies drenched around its wick,
and through the bamboo curtains
life cycles of stars shed their old light,

travel as one response
to reach this room, where they lie silent
without any pretense of fuel or wings.

Let the Cold Come

Already it shines in trees
holding seeds, festers
on sloping roof tops
not yet embossed with frostwork.
Already the apples redden
on their espalier, the children
think a little more and harder.
The old grow slowly older—
a kind of moss creeps
into our blood, green on red,
red on green—complementary—
either way it happens.
Not to say time slows:
it quickens. Not to say
we aren't grateful to have had
a summer as long and hot
as hell. We are. Not to imply
we'll miss the berries
slipping into our palms.
As if they'd been waiting
on the bush for some kind
of furless, all too human
hunger—for the brush of skin
against skin—that signal
old as the first fall, when
Adam led the cowering
Eve away, behind them
Paradise bursting into flame.

Floyd Skloot

Born in Brooklyn in 1947, he is the author of 18 books. He is a creative nonfiction writer, poet, and fiction writer whose work has received three Pushcart Prizes, a Pen USA Literary Award, two Pacific NW Book Awards, an Independent Publishers Book Award, and two Oregon Book Awards. His writing has appeared in such distinguished magazines as *The New York Times Magazine, Atlantic Monthly, Harper's, Poetry, American Scholar, Georgia Review, Sewanee Review, Southern Review, Hudson Review, Gettysburg Review, Boulevard, Virginia Quarterly Review, Prairie Schooner,* and *Creative Nonfiction*. His books include the memoirs *In the Shadow of Memory, A World of Light,* and *The Wink of the Zenith: The Shaping of a Writer's Life*; the poetry collections *Approximately Paradise, The End of Dreams, Selected Poems: 1970-2005,* and *The Snow's Music*; and the novels *Summer Blue* and *Patient 002*. His newest books include his first collection of short stories, *Cream of Kohlrabi*, and a forthcoming collection of poems, *Close Reading*. He co-edited *The Best American Science Writing 2011* with his daughter, Rebecca Skloot. He contributes book reviews to the *New York Times Book Review, Boston Globe, Philadelphia Inquirer, Los Angeles Times, Harvard Review, Sewanee Review, Notre Dame Review* and other publications, and is a member of the National Book Critics Circle. He lives in Portland, Oregon with his wife, Beverly Hallberg, a weaver and landscape painter, whose light-filled works cross between impressionistic and abstracted styles. Her paintings grace the covers of Floyd's books. More can be found at:
http://www.floydskloot.com

The Fiddler's Trance
> *after Chagall*

The air above Vitebsk was filled with Jews
gassed green. From the synagogues and orchards,
rubble of butcher shops, from crushed forges,
charred barns, and wooden huts rose the blues
and blazing yellows of the world to come.
Red footprints racing nowhere across snow
were chased by spirals of dark fire that no
one saw in time. Every bird was struck dumb
by dawn. Chagall remembered the future
before ever leaving home. Yet he knew
song was possible. Whatever was true
about the sound of night, he would picture
one lonely fiddler looming and entranced
to find himself the center of a dance.

Starry Night
> *Perhaps I might really recover if I were in the country for a time.*
> —*Vincent Van Gogh*

Tonight the moon throbs with light
it seizes from stars as they rise
and the cypresses grow holy
before my eyes. Wind fills the sky.
I see clouds shudder, houses
and shops cower, but somehow
high grass finds its own source
of stillness. I think it is violet
in nature. Never has there
been such a night for seeing
how the dark world thrives
when day's brilliance dies
and sight fully becomes surprise.

Who would want all these deep blues
to soften as though toward dawn?
No dawn will bring along
a day as pure again. Who would
want to be well enough to lose
such hues? I know a man can
be so far from madness the true
world cannot find him. I know
he will be saved only when
the moon collects enough radiance
to render heaven tangible
as the breath of sunflowers.

Look: there is a glow inside
the emptiest spaces when we
study their darkness. There is
also a hush no stroke of
a painter's brush can muffle.
Think of the instant swallows
rising above a field you enter
suddenly loop back in unison—
a thick landscape of faith
that is beyond words, yet explains
why I am standing here at all.

Yeshiva in the Pale, January, 1892

Early morning as Cossacks on horseback
circled the old wooden synagogue, chants
seeped out like smoke through the walls. Black
hated elders inside shut their eyes and danced
in circles of their own before the holy ark.
Prayer deepened the air as one fat soldier nailed
the Tsar's seal to the door: CLOSED. Then a spark
cast from somewhere near the rising sun sailed

across the wintery sky, encircling soldier
and temple, nuzzling rooftree, gable, beam,
It found the place where mingled rage and dream
were draft enough to let a wildfire smolder.
One moment shadows questioned the winter dark
and next moment the answer arrived in flame.

Lee Slonimsky

Born in New York City in 1951, his second book of poems, *Pythagoras in Love*, is a sonnet sequence of which the poet A. E. Stallings has written, "the sonnet turns out to be the perfect—maybe even the Platonic—form for Lee Slonimsky's Pythagorean meditations." His latest book, *Logician of the Wind*, features 40 sonnets alongside poems in other forms and free verse. His poems have appeared in numerous publications, including *The Carolina Quarterly*, *Connecticut Review*, *Measure*, *The New York Times*, *North Dakota Quarterly*, *Poetry Daily*, and *32 Poems*. He also manages a hedge fund, Ocean Partners LP.

Burial of the Sun

What hieroglyphs trees' leafy shadows form,
upon a meadow glassbright with the gold
demands of sinking sun upon the warm
blue remnants of a summer day grown old.

Pythagoras can calculate how long
before the sun inters itself once more.
The angled math of shadow's never wrong,
and neither is hypotenuse of soar,

triangulation by ascending hawk,
whose broadwinged glide appears to climb the light.
But how to measure, on his evening walk,
the loss of his brief days to endless night.

A final gleam of bronze enshrines this day.
He ponders brevity. Goes on his way.

The Menorah Tree

Its curving branches: candelabra-like.
Remarkable, how treeshape is an art
of evolution. Maybe there's an Ark
in nearby grove of leafy oaks. Let's look.

But though we walk the rest of that slow day,
Menorah Tree is singular.

                      Deny
a deity—conversely, kneel and pray—
the tree is there both ways, with orange sky
an inkling of the sun's eternal flame,
or almost so. Sun dies well down the road
but much to bask in, if for now. My name
and those of forebears and descendents fades
yet something's in the coldest wind that lasts,
that sources tangled roots in the deep past.

Adam Sol

Born in New York in 1969, he is the author of three books of poetry, including *Jeremiah, Ohio*, a novel in poems which was shortlisted for Ontario's Trillium Award for Poetry; and *Crowd of Sounds*, which won the award in 2004. He has also published essays and reviews for *The Globe and Mail*, *The Forward*, *Critique*, and *Studies in Jewish American Literature*. Originally from Connecticut, he teaches at Laurentian University's campus in Barrie, Ontario and lives in Toronto with his wife, Rabbi Yael Splansky, and their three sons.

Newark Local

Lord, I am weary as an old mop.

I have nearly emptied my pockets
       and spent my last—no.

Enough! Begone, crowd canker!
       Away, weariness and grief!

There is already too much tragedy on the Turnpike today.
       I will withhold my contribution.

See how even the exit signs plead and pulse.

Yea, though my heart burns and my neck
       creaks and cracks,
       yet will I urge, cajole, bluster and muster.

For indeed we are a holy people.
yea, see our hodgepodge and hullabaloo.

We have built more cities on hills
       than all the ants of the Amazon.

But we still do not know the path to righteousness,
> o my soul.

Those who say so are false teeth and toupees.

Behold we are lonely emperors.
> We are coyotes in strip malls.
> > We are lost bees.

Send us your wisdom and discretion, o lord.
> Renew us as in the days of old—

Not as they were, but as we imagined them.

Onna Solomon

Born in East Lansing, Michigan in 1979, her writing has appeared in *Beloit Poetry Journal*, *Denver Quarterly*, *Cimarron Review*, and *32 Poems*, among others. She received her Masters in creative writing from Boston University, and now lives and works in Ann Arbor, Michigan. In her free time, she organizes community art events through the Huron River Arts Initiative.

Before my Uncle's Death

Inside the cramped hospital room we all
laughed hard—his wife and daughter both, his niece
and sister joining in until our mad
cackling cracked our faces flush open.

It had been days. Across the old man's head
a line of silver staples showed where they
had tried to stop the brain-bleed. Rob, his son,
had stayed awake two nights and now he slept—

not even our laughter could stir them though
our sounds were like the shrill cacophony
of Jewish minstrels (the Irish call them 'keeners'),
those mourners hired to wail after the coffin.

The morning's brutal light slit through the blinds,
slashed across their faces as Robbie sank
deeper into his chair, his body slumped
beside the bed where Uncle Al lay dying.

We laughed at them and couldn't stop—Rob's jaw
dropped down to match his father's hollow gape—
their syncopated snore and wheeze pronounced
a comic discord, an absurd duet.

Melissa Stein

Born in Philadelphia, she is the author of the poetry collection *Rough Honey*, winner of the 2010 APR/Honickman First Book Prize. Her poems have appeared in *Southern Review*, *Harvard Review*, *Best New Poets 2009*, *New England Review*, and many other journals and anthologies. She has received fellowships from Yaddo, the MacDowell Colony, the Bread Loaf Writers' Conference, and the Djerassi Resident Artists Program, and her work has won awards from *Spoon River Poetry Review*, *Literal Latté*, and the Dorothy Sargent Rosenberg Foundation, among others. She is a freelance editor and writer in San Francisco.
http://www.melissastein.com

Olives, Bread, Honey, and Salt

The lanes are littered with the bodies of bees.
A torrent took them, swarming in branches
just as the white buds loosened their hearts
of pale yellow powder. Each body is a lover:
the one with skin blank as pages; the one
so moved by the pulse ticking in your throat;
the one who took your lips in his teeth
and wouldn't let go; the one who turned
from you and lay there like a carcass. If we were
made to be whole, we wouldn't be so lost
to each offering of tenderness and a story.
Therefore our greatest longing is our home.
There is always the one bee that circles and circles,
twitching its sodden wings.

Halo

A swirl of it: a stain, like cinnamon:
that's how it was, at the base
of her skull, radiating like a halo.
I watched, for a long time, her outline,
her shadow, her second self
sink into sand. They say the soul
lifts from the body; that it takes wing
from sullied matter, a perfumed storm,
petals and light. I saw a slackening,
a gradual collapse to paleness tinged
in yellow, in slate. A lowering, not a lifting
as the earth that once held her up
loosened to take her in. A sigh.
Then a quiet that was more than quiet,
a listening that itself became like noise.

Want Me

Lemons crystallized in sugar, glistening
on a blue-glazed plate. The rarest volume
bound in blood leather. A silk carpet
woven so finely you can't push a needle through,
that from one edge is the silver of a leaf
underwater, and from the other bleu lumière,
first frost on the cornflowers. A duet for cello
and woodsmoke, violin and icicle. Tangle of
black hair steeped in sandalwood, jasmine,
bergamot and vetiver and jewelled
with pomegranate seeds. Panther's broad tongue
soothing hunt-bruised paws. Eyelids of ribbonsnakes.
Taut skin of a lavender crème brûlée. Split
vanilla pods swollen with bourbon. A luna
moth's wings, enormous, celadon, trembling.

Nomi Stone

Born in Los Angeles in 1981, she is currently a Ph.D candidate in Cultural Anthropology at Columbia University. Her first book of poems, *Stranger's Notebook*, chronicles her time living in one of the last cohesive Jewish communities in North Africa. She has a Masters in Middle Eastern Studies from Oxford University, and was a Fulbright scholar in creative writing in Tunisia.

The Fall of the First Temple, 586 B.C., Jerusalem

The priests buzzed around the nothing
that was left there, inspecting it with
itching fingers. One threw the useless
keys into the everything above. Now,

they must learn to make
a meadow a temple, an act or an absence of
an act, a temple. They weep and then
become their altar.

Outside of Time

During the Sabbath you are in other time. You carry nothing
but your continuing

breath. Enter here, where
time is not

time, inside an alignment of the heavenly
and earthly worlds. The same happens when two bodies

join: the worlds rowing under each
skin climb into a zygote. Birth. And then no-time again

when the ram's horn
possesses your walled village. The men

blow the horn on each day of rest—

when you hear it, you stop
your breath and wish.

Listen. Your breath
held.

        And those stars
        behind the stars you recognize,

they stay.

Lisa Gluskin Stonestreet

Born in Stockton, California in 1968, she is the author of *Tulips, Water, Ash,* selected for the Morse Poetry Prize and published by University Press of New England in 2009. After working as a technical editor, arts magazine publisher, gift wrapper, film studio gofer, English instructor, and cocktail waitress, Lisa now makes her living as a freelance editor. Her poems have been awarded a Javits fellowship and a Phelan Award, and have appeared in journals such as *32 Poems, Quarterly West, Blackbird, The Iowa Review, Third Coast,* and *Best New Poets* 2005 and 2006. She lives in San Francisco with her husband and son.
http://www.lisagluskinstonestreet.com/blog

De Profundis

out of the depths I cry to you, O Lord

—more like out of the middle, the soft
chewy center of *here*: the mailbox,
the toaster, the dentist office: I cry

to you, or to nothing, I whisper
and roll my eyes: *Oh, lord.*
        O Lord. Forgive us

our dailiness, our lists of lists.
The gearshift work, the newspaper cutouts,
coupons and cashback in the slow lane.

Whiteboard, whiteout. Little yellow
notes everywhere like moths.
        Oh, lord. Remember

us, here: the soft warm milky middle,
its erasing breath, its easy arms. Here
where we lie, mostly and meanwhile.

Jars

These last weeks, so many
        things, just so much and all the mason jars
                filling up with light and oddments, lids off

for everything rolling around in there:
        car and computer crashes (minor), your twisted ankle,
                a marriage (ours), trail of ants swirling

down into the cat dish, basil and dandelions
        leaping up in the yard: What did I think
                would happen? We were transformed,

and obstinate. The phone kept ringing. A bruise
        on my thigh from the suitcase, another
                mid-forearm, shape of a thumb

in brown and blue. New sheets
        on the neighbor's line. I paid bills, juggled
                money and packages. Could not stop

smiling, shivering all at once. Yesterday
        someone left a ring of soft blue pebbles
                on the front steps, where the bus pauses

on its way to the beach. I took out the trash,
        took a call from a friend (her mother's throat
                ringed with tumor). Back in bed, shivering,

then the morning, held down and arching
        toward you. Three jars on the dresser:
                tulips, water, ash.

Marcela Sulak

Born in El Campo, Texas in 1968, she worked in South America and Central Europe, and, most recently, in Washington, DC. For the last 14 months she has been directing the Shaindy Rudoff Graduate Program in Creative Writing at Bar-Ilan University in Israel. Her books include *Immigrant* and the chapbook *Of All The Things That Don't Exist, I Love You Best*. She has translated three collections of poetry from the Czech Republic and Congo-Zaire. Her poems have appeared in *Guernica*, *Poet Lore*, *The Notre Dame Review*, *The South East Review*, and *No Tell Motel*, among others.

Pomelo with Fallen Angel

Sealed inside this yellow peel, beneath the heavy
compressed clouds they call white skin, the wings
are bound and pressed. So when she feels the knife
she quivers, when the skin's peeled back, oh ecstasy.
Yet when the wings are lifted out, they're different
than they were before; instead of wind they're filled
with water, sweet and bitter, each feather fitted
to a narrow juice-filled sac.
                                    They look like
the hands of an unripe bride, pale from waiting
in the dark, long slender fingers reaching,
ever unmet. Even if they were to dry a little
in the sun, like cicadas falling out before
they grow into their souls, these wings
won't rise—they left in such a rush. And she
has never learned wane and billow, what has tides,
and what a spoon is for. The wet pomelo feathers
wink like the seven hundred eyes of flies
and scatter like dew, and here she is,
opening her mouth.

Jerusalem

In the covered shuk an orange was the only source of light,
the spices snored in canvass bags all night in Jerusalem.

There are always scored stones above, curtains, flags below,
shifting their gravity from shoe to shoe in tight-fitting Jerusalem.

The cracks in the Western Wall are soaked in prayers,
the doves are scraps of light above Jerusalem.

The Mount of Olives crouches over the Wailing Wall:
bleached bone, bleached stone, sun-crumbled white Jerusalem.

Like teeth broken on what they've been given to say,
rows and rows of white boxes, asleep against the might of Jerusalem.

Bullet holes are horizontal, rain-bored holes are vertical.
The pools, the ritual baths fill themselves in the sight of Jerusalem.

No other city has drunk so much ink;
who from the sages would know how to write, but for Jerusalem?

Ecclesiastes

It's so nice to be pretty on Eli Cohen Street
in Katamon, Jerusalem and wearing polka dots
on a swinging dress with a small cinched waist
pushing a blue-eyed golden child through
the trade winds in her pram. The trees
are swaying, and on the bench below them
an old woman looks up through the boughs
to a parcel of clouds, when she sees us she smiles.
When we pass she stands up and begins with her
zlata moje, my golden child, and she reaches to
touch our cheeks and her hand stays outstretched
and she's asking for just a little of our gold, something
for the bus or for lunch or, I reach into my tiny purse,
drop some coins, since now her hand
is the meter that keeps the world running,
that turns us in our slot.

Pia Taavila

Born in Walled Lake, Michigan in 1952, she now lives in Fredericksburg, Virginia. She teaches literature and creative writing at Gallaudet University in Washington, DC. Her collection of poems, *Moon on the Meadow*, was published in 2008 by Gallaudet University Press, and *Two Winters*, a chapbook, was published in December 2011 by Finishing Line Press. Her poems have appeared in such journals as *The Bear River Review, Appalachian Heritage, The Comstock Review, Threepenny Review, Birmingham Poetry Review, StorySouth, The Asheville Poetry Review, 32 Poems, Measure, Ibbetson Street Review,* and *The Southern Review*, among others. She is also a frequent participant at the Bear River, Sewanee and Key West Literary conferences.

Lost

Out on Lake Huron, I raise the keel,
tie down jibs, lash the spar and rudder.
The anchor reels out on its heavy chain.
My radio rasps as a gull climbs overhead,
immune to matters of heart and hand.
Board games and jigsaw puzzles,
their pieces gone missing, line the shelves.
The galley's loaded with provisions,
but no beneficence lies on board,
the first mate's absence obvious.
I look at weather maps, arrowed charts,
the sky, and try to set a forward destination.
There's nowhere to go, no fish to lure
as the sun slowly slides beneath
the waterline: shores of vapor, haze.

Yom Kippur

In the autumn garden,
I chop away dead yucca spires,
their white bell blossoms distant
in memory. My fingers comb ivy
and vinca for fallen leaves that crumble
in my hands. I think of crimes
against my loved ones, count my sins,
pull at spider webs and chickweed,
stubborn at the root.

I make my piles, gather the detritus
of trees into bags set against the curb.
I sweep the sidewalk, edge a trowel's
blade beneath a hardy clutch of clover.
Even in drought, the barely living cling
like runners on a fencepost, adamant.
My roses, staked and tied to the wire mesh,
wilt on the stalk, feebly pink. Still,
honeysuckle persists, fragrant, wild,
and berries will ripen in the winter to come.

Philip Terman

Born in Cleveland in 1957, he now lives outside of Grove City, Philadelphia with his wife Christine Hood and daughters Miriam and Bella. His books of poetry include *The House of Sages*, *Book of the Unbroken Days*, *Rabbis of the Air*, and *The Torah Garden*. His poems have appeared in many journals and anthologies, including *Poetry*, *The Georgia Review*, *The Forward*, *The Autumn House Anthology of Contemporary Poetry*, and *Blood to Remember: American Poets on the Holocaust*. Recipient of the Kenneth Patchen Award, the Sow's Ear Chapbook Prize, and the Anna Davidson Rosenberg Award for Poetry on the Jewish Experience, he teaches creative writing and literature at Clarion University of Pennsylvania. Terman co-directs the Chautauqua Writers' Festival and is Contributing Editor for Poetry for the journal *Chautauqua*.

The Shank Bone

Our dog swipes the shank bone from the sedar plate,
shakes her muzzle from side to side, takes off
through Elijah's door: this roasted symbol of the sacrificial

lamb we offered in the Temple to remember our exile
and commemorate our liberation now clenched
in the jaws of this overgrown golden retriever puppy,

this what-we-call-in-Hebrew *zeroah*, meaning "arm,"
meaning how our God outstretched his enormous arm
to help his people in our times of aggravation, what

we're undergoing now, the guests arrived, the table
set with plates and wine glasses, *Haggadahs* and candles,
bowl of salt water, bowl of roasted eggs, the *charosete*—

our laborious mortar—chopped and set beside the bitter
herbs, what we will mix in with our dog's Alpo once
we can coerce her to give it up, but she's clamping

and sloshing it around her drenched tongue as if
this were the last bone on earth, as if she understood
that this was from the original lamb our High Priest chose

when we all put down our weapons and tools to gather
and witness this primordial offering: to assuage our guilt,
to accommodate our primitive desires, to draw nearer

to the source, our surrendering—before the destruction
and therefore absence of our assigned place
so the scholars say we can sacrifice nowhere

until the source returns and now my five-year-old daughter
has tackled our dog in the yard and pulls hard at the bone,
all of our guests approaching closer in mesmerized silence.

The Famous Jewish Russian-Woman Poet Termanovsky

If you found out your great grandmother
was a poet, if there was one obscure book
you discovered one off-day at the bottom

of a dusty cardboard box, in the corner
basement room, covered up by pickle jars,
slid behind your father's war uniforms,

a volume slim as a small hand, the cover
a faded blue, layered and sealed with mold,
the pages tearing with a touch, the letters

in Yiddish, and there's her name: Termanovsky—
your name, before shortened by the authorities,
the way they'd slice off anything unpronounceable.

Termanovsky: the famous Russian-Jewish woman
poet, her daguerreotype on the title's facing page,
her face, the one you recognize from worn photos,

but younger, a beauty, no babushka—a frilled scarf
wrapped around the neck, her dark thick hair
flowing from beneath a tilted-to-one-side beret,

a few strands loose across her cheeks, dangling
from her lips a cigarette. You examine the strange
letters, lines, stanzas, wonder about

the pressure of her fingers pressing the pen
to the paper, between the poverty and the pogrom,
the praying for a relative to sponsor her over,

the baking of the bread she had to peddle
in the marketplace, having to worry about who
would print and publish poems by a woman

named Termanovsky, about being a girl
in the shtetl, the smell of herring and challa
rising, horses and wagons in the open air,

the mud streets, the learned huddled toward
the eastern wall, old men in black coats, how
it shamed her to have to sit on her side

of the synagogue—even if she had the space,
even if she had the time to save her moments
in words, the way she kept buttons in a box,

and was assured of the support to write them all down.

The Raccoon

Because our corn stalks were mangled—
some toppled over completely—

and the cobs nibbled and hacked
through their fiber sheaths,

and because my wife's father, the expert—
the one who, past seventy, still traps beaver

and hauls them to his pond when he wants
a dam built—examined the barn

and discovered a "peck of poop in there,"
causing my five-year old daughter

to laugh hysterically and repeat all day,
"a peck of poop, a peck of poop,"

and because that same father-in-law
agreed to loan us his hand-built trap,

twice the size of a bread box,
all steel and secure handle, and

because my wife—ever resourceful—
concocted a poison of bait consisting

of matzo—the bread, it turned out,
of its affliction—and peanut butter,

and because when I first tried to lift
the cage with the weight of his body

he hissed and swiped his claws, scraping
the air a few inches from my hand,

and I jumped against the house,
swinging the door back and slamming it

into my wife's face, who in turn
leaped and felled my daughter,

I found myself steering this pacing
beast that would, if it could escape

from the towel-covered cage
in the hatchback of my Subaru, tear

right through my bones before my foot
could reach the gas pedal, before

the bumpy ride down the gravel road
to the game lands could wind through

the morning, before in that confused moment
we could plan better lives for ourselves.

That Lightness

Tossing my daughter into the air,
black hair tussled, arms and legs
splayed out like a cat's in flight,
part thrill, part fear, the outburst

of joy, lost in abandonment,
that small space just beneath
the rough-cut pine joists supporting
the exposed ceiling, which is,

during the flicker of her visit, heaven,
if what we mean has something to do
with bliss, escape from the body,
such as the ache my arms feel now

when I catch her in my clasped,
half-open, ready-and-waiting palms
and pull her towards my chest
that's pounding from its own thrill

and fear of possible failure
--the imagined fall and chaos after--
our two faces against each other's,
hers wide-eyed and grinning,

mine whatever astonishment
looks like, both flushed with the blood
of the moment, and she enunciates
the password: *mo'?*--her parlance

for more, let's go, why are we pausing
when we could have perfection?--
and I fling her up again, each exertion
enflaming my burning muscles.

What parent wouldn't risk self-
combustion to keep their child
from one elation to another?
Isn't that our mission,

to be the force that swings them
like a rope from tree to tree
above our daily catastrophes,
our absurd predicaments,

our private obsessions? And,
let's admit it to ourselves,
don't we believe that if we continue
throwing them back they will keep

with them a little of that thinner air
and live their lives with some knowledge
of the infinite, that lightness, a space
we ourselves could never reach?

Carine Topal

Born in New York City in 1949, she attended New York University and has lived in Israel and worked with Russian and Morrocan immigrants in Beit Shimush, Jerusalem. Her work has appeared in many journals, such as *Caliban, Greensboro Review, Pacific Review,* POOL, *Oberon, Water~Stone Review,* and many others. Her three collections of poems include: *God As Thief, Bed Of Want,* for which she won the Robert G. Cohn Prose Poetry Award, and *In The Heaven Of Never Before.* She is the recipient of residences at Hedgebrook and the Summer Literary Seminars, was nominated for a Pushcart Prize, and won many poetry contests, including the Robert G. Cohen Prose Poetry Award and the Jane Kenyon Poetry Prize. Currently she teaches poetry and memoir writing in private workshops in Redondo Beach, California and in La Quinta, California.

Veering
for Rene

1.
Within the waters of the planet
his is the face I see

because he came back and held me
and I held on in the bay of closely

parked cars, a small inventory
of shining rafts, unmoored.

Of all that stood between us
there was only the risk he took in speaking,

and his human weight, which he turned
toward me, his head leaning to the west,

mine, safely nested in the crook
of his arm. Facing east.

2.

Of all that stood between us
there was only the risk in speaking,

and his human weight, spilling
toward me, his head leaning to the west,

mine, safely nested in the crook
of his arm, eastward.

Within the waters of the planet
we are among the not-yet-drowning,

because he came back, held me, and I held on
in the bay of closely parked cars,

a small inventory of shining rafts,
unmoored.

Rachel Trousdale

Born in New Haven, Conneticut in 1975, she is an associate professor of English at Agnes Scott College in Decatur, Georgia, where she teaches twentieth century literature and creative writing. Her poems have appeared or are forthcoming in *Literary Imagination*, the *Atlanta Review*, the *Southern Poets Anthology*, *Natural Bridge*, and *Confrontation*, among other places. Her critical book *Nabokov, Rushdie, and the Transnational Imagination* was published by Palgrave Macmillan in 2010, and she is now working on a book on humor in twentieth century American poetry.

The New Synagogue in Prague

is yellow, baroque, and recently restored.
Large signs request abstention
from videography. The man beside me
films them. My mother's family
came from Hamburg, six hours
north and west from here.
My grandfather was born outside New York,
making it strange to find his name among
the list of Prague's deported
stenciled on the wall in fresh gold leaf.
Later, outside the graveyard gate,
the videographer's Israeli wife
scolds me—I don't know to wash my hands.

God Instructs Man to Name the Animals

Who are you, ridiculous biped,
inefficiently haired, dulled with spots,
to assign to my creatures a few
ill-observed syllables;
to living muscle and inventive spark, "dolphin";
to the irritable, hungry quest for perfection, "orb spider";
to avid, sleepy ruthlessness, "cat"?
The more you say, the more you insult:
the naked mole rat takes his tunnels for clothing,
the splendid quetzal is more to you than to his mate
reduced to feathers. They have their names but need no names;
this goat knows that he is this goat;
the wolf, that the scents he lives by
are echoing in his own nose.
But name them anyway. To you
who are only a syllable,
whose claws break when you scrabble for roots,
who lacking fur must steal other people's fur,
any skin is better than your own skin;
wrap yourself up in "mink," "ermine," "fox,"
using the only real weapons I gave you.

Emily Warn

Born in San Francisco in 1953, she moved at the age of seven from the then Bohemian neighborhood in Marin, California to the Orthodox Jewish community in Detroit. For Warn, poetry links music and meaning every bit as powerfully and oddly as religious traditions do, inventing complicated, invisible relations. She moved to the Pacific Northwest in 1978 to work for North Cascades National Park, and a year later moved to Seattle, where she has lived more or less ever since. Warn has published five collections of poetry, including three books: *The Leaf Path*, *The Novice Insomniac*, and *Shadow Architect*, all from Copper Canyon Press. She most recently served as the Webby Award–winning founding editor of poetryfoundation.org, and now divides her time between Seattle and Twisp, Washington.

The Rabbi Stumbles

The congregation watches stunned,
quiet for once, when the rabbi
loses his place in the Torah.

Nobody shifts in folding metal chairs.
No men bend inside prayer shawls to gossip.
No women comment about last night's Shabbas meal.

The rabbi is bending his head over the Torah
and weeping. A tear falls on the goat-skin parchment,
trailing across Hebrew words like rowboat's wake.

The congregation knows no law, no blessing,
for when a rabbi cries and cries and cannot speak.
Will his tears wash away the words of the Torah?

Will they erase the delicate balance between letter
and number? Did God whisper a saying in his ear
so holy it cannot be spoken?

Or does he see the blindness of all rabbis?
The congregation fidgets, then hears
its impatience and is ashamed.

The Torah cannot help them. the morning schedule
of prayers does not include his sorrow. They know
they cannot continue without a word from God.

The little girl watches the yellowish-orange light
falling through the cheap stained-glass windows.
She smells her grandfather's leathery teflin;

the faint cigar smoke o his lips.
She reaches her hand into his roomy pockets,
feels their absolute comfort slipping away,

because the rabbi, a grown man, cannot stop crying.
In silence, her grandfather knows the girl's place.

While the Secretaries Compose the Engineers' Torah

They want a chance at solitaire, the version played
on screen. they like the dealer's impersonal hum,
how he shuffles the blank display into flashing
diamonds and queens. The secretaries hope for a straight run
to five o'clock, a solid half-hour of good luck before
the boss intervenes or the fax scrolls out its orders.

All morning, the secretaries transcribe inspection reports:
the weather at 8 a.m. on November 10th—cloudy, cool
with sun breaks. the crew bolted the centrifugal pump
to the dry well, dug a biofiltration swale,
and covered the sewer line with native fill.
the secretaries dream with their headphones o
while the words fit into place: the water main
installation is fifty percent complete, the correct grade
achieved at such a such time on such a such date,
the feat inscribed in case the company stands accused
of design flaws, faulty procedures, or improperly cured cement.

The secretaries impatiently wait to exit Word
and enter the command for Dice. perhaps today
they'll receive a stacked deck, a numerical sequence
to marvel at. They pray for no business until five,
when they can check out from checking out
the electronic dealer who arranges their cards.

Joshua Weiner

Born in Boston in 1963, he is the author of *The World's Room, From the Book of Giants*, and the forthcoming *The Figure of a Man Being Swallowed by a Fish*. He is the editor of *At The Barriers: On The Poetry of Thom Gunn*. A recipient of a Whiting Writers Award and the Rome Prize, he teaches at University of Maryland and lives in Washington, DC.

Psalm

When I sing to you I am alone these days
        and can't believe it, as if the stars

—while gazing up at them—just shut off.
        Astonished:

I search out the one light, brightest light
        in the night sky, but find

I cannot find it without weaker lights to guide me
        like red tail-lights on a car up ahead

after midnight when I'm sleepy, that illustrate
        how the highway curves,

curving to a hook, and maybe save my life
        and it means nothing to me

because nothing has happened, not the faintest
        glint of drama.

(Raining gently, the tarmac turns slick, moistened
        to life with renewed residues;

I can sense it with my hands on the wheel,
        the drops—not too heavy—

drumming off-time rhythms on the metal roof,
> the metal surface like a skin tense and sweating

and the road empty now, there are so many
> exits ...)

Where is my family, both hearth and constellated trail of flicker
> I have always followed to your word?

There, but mastered by fear of dark compulsions
> and loathing atrocities committed in your name,

they hit the dimmer switch and extinguish themselves
> whenever I sing your praises...

Who can blame them?
> (I can't help but blame them.)

And anyway they are far from me
> (farthest when they come to visit)—

I should be self-reliant, in my armchair
> like Emerson reading by a single lamp;

I should not need them, finding in you
> myself, little firebug needing no outlet,

my soft light blinking as I oxidize my aimless flight
> to love, to the good,

even my glowing chemistry unnecessary now
> in the ultimate light of day.

But what good would that do me?
> With you, in you, perhaps others do not matter,

but this isn't heaven, and I cannot make a circle
> all on my own—

Photon, luciferin, meteor: as I burn myself
> to pieces, I only pray

    let my sparking tail remain a moment longer
          than our physics might allow,

    some indication, however brief, that there continues
          (amen) a path to follow.

Henry Weinfield

Born in Montreal in 1949, he is now professor of Liberal Studies and English at the University of Notre Dame. His recent books are *A Wandering Aramaean: Passover Poems and Translations* and *The Blank-Verse Tradition from Milton to Stevens: Freethinking and the Crisis of Modernity*, and *Without Mythologies: New and Selected Poems and Translations*, *The Music of Thought in the Poetry of George Oppen and William Bronk*, and a translation, made in collaboration with Catherine Schlegel, of Hesiod's *Theogony and Works and Days*. His translation of and commentary on the *Collected Poems* of Stéphane Mallarmé was published by the University of California Press in 1995. His latest collection, *A Wandering Aramaean: Passover Poems and Translations*, was published by Dos Madres Press in 2012.

Hebrew Melodies

I The Wanderer

>*All the rivers run into the sea; yet the sea is not full…*
>Ecclesiastes 1:7

Slowly the seasons circle and converge.
Summer's assumptions fall beneath the surge
Of wind that widens in its withering.
Late-winter blurring into early-spring
Summons the Wanderer in his own blood,
Bursts through whatever bulwarks had withstood
The pulse of passion rushing to the void—
Till all delineations are destroyed.

Why should the Wanderer pursue his course,
Season by season, searching for a source,
And slowly circle like an old refrain

From east to west and west to east again—
Summer to autumn; autumn, winter; spring—
If nothing comes of all his wandering?

He sees the seasons circling back once more,
And nothing is as it has been before
Upon the lands and in the skies and seas;
He sees how in their superfluities
They seize the allotted moment and withdraw,
Accommodated to the common law
That binds them up as sheaves beneath the sun
And sweeps them out—into oblivion.

Our life is error, then, the Wanderer says.
It bears us fiercely forward through the days,
Faithful to some unerring symmetry.
Green burns gold and burnishes to red,
And imperceptibly is blurred and bled,
Falling at last beneath the ancient tree.

II My Father Was a Wandering Aramaean

…you shall make this response before the Lord your God: "A wandering Aramaean was my father, he went down into Egypt and lived there as an alien, few in number, and there he became a great nation, mighty and populous."
    Deuteronomy 26:5

My father was a wandering Aramaean,
Bordering upon the Gentile and the Jew.
The promised land was never his to stay in,
He had no church or synagogue to pray in—
Music was the religion that he knew.

My father was a wandering Aramaean,
Enlightened by the darkness that he found.
He never lifted a triumphal paean:
No one is chosen—Hebrew, Greek, or pagan—
The self-same cloud encompasses us round.

My father was a wandering Aramaean,
Not reconciled or reconcilable.
Whether in Egypt or the deep Judaean
Plain, or Sheol where the shades complain,
The rigor of his refusals rings out still.

III Without Mythologies

Without mythologies the leaves are blown
Hither and yon, seeds sown and flowers grown:
They do it on their own without mythologies.

Without mythologies they wax and wane,
Neither complain nor hasten to explain,
Since everything is plain without mythologies.

Without mythologies when day is done
Under the sun, songs sung and races run,
A new one is begun without mythologies.

Karen Weiser

Born in Nyack, New York in 1975, she is a mother, poet, and doctoral candidate at the CUNY Graduate Center, studying early American literature. She lives in New York City and has taught literature at St. John's University and Barnard College. A Norma Faber First Book Award Finalist, *To Light Out* is her first full-length collection.

A Person Sits Next to a Fugue

A person sits next to a world of possibilities
leaving the latch unlocked—
I have a question about fugues
but I'm embarrassed to ask it
while the weather's on the bounce
as if all other things being don't
the fugue appears through the unlocked window
as omnipotent as the horizon's 360
rising like a struggling would-be fabled bridge
like the fog of a Jewish New Year
quite slippable in hypotheticals
cables and the long space of above-water air

A person sits next to a world of almost situations
making a living as a memoir
thoroughfares fill with drizzle scrambling
progressive strangers with their ding eyes
I am sure a fugue is near
in the almost-echo of park benches—
this is not the city of the blessed worker
Americana seduction like original face paint
reflected in a gridiron puddle.

Rachel Wetzsteon

Born in Manhattan in 1967, she passed away in 2009 after joining *The New Republic* as poetry editor. She received degrees from Yale University, Johns Hopkins University, and Columbia University. She made her home in the Morningside Heights neighborhood of New York, which is the setting for many of her poems. She published three collections of poetry, including the National Poetry Series winner *The Other Stars*, *Home and Away*, and *Sakura Park*, as well as *Influential Ghosts*, a critical study of poet W. H. Auden.

May Pole
in memory of Sarah Hannah

Sarah, the night I learned of you
the Spanish sunset split in two:
since then I've been looking through

blurred windows at a warring sky
where violent crimson tendrils vie
with wisps of light that madly try

to hold onto their fragile piece
of vault despite the fierce increase
of red that lacks the heart to cease.

You know too well the frail tightrope
between grand plan and slender hope,
scanned buoy, arm and heliotrope

as fish inspect thin strips of sand;
you could not live on this parched land.
But, dear friend fallen, understand

I will not let the velvety
encroachments declare victory;
I will not let the memory

of all your strength and wild delight
be made one micro-beam less bright
by all the bullies of the night.

Instead I'll cast into the air
a picture of your frank wry stare,
a locket of your golden hair,

your poem about the salad days,
and watch these souvenirs amaze
the scarlet henchmen of sad ways

who carved such trenches in your mind
but cannot touch the brilliant, kind
and joyful trace you left behind

or find me nursing the belief
that red's a ruler, not a thief
ruthless in its lust for grief.

Vanished gorse-girl, my first urge is
to despair, but rawness merges
with resolve, and so my dirge is:

let's stare at the setting sun,
hazard an opinion
of who has lost and who has won;

let's regard her lasting spark
and tell the tyrants of the dark
who has left the greater mark.

Six Leagues Under

Unlike the sharks who, if they want
to stay alive must stay in motion,
some prey upon the very young
in the deep folds of the ocean.

I'd sat upon the beach so long
that even the lifeguard, bored ingrate,
fell asleep thinking doubtful starfish
and skittish crabs were my dry fate.

But suddenly, I've plunged into water
without wading or warning to guide me in.
You prick me. I bleed and am so madly happy,
but now comes the wait for the terrible fin.

Apologies to an Ambulance

The red light was my racing heart,
the siren my pain made public,
and the body inside, a study in scarlet,
was battered yet somehow grotesquely pretty.
I drew a rosy curtain over the city.
But the naked city went on bleeding, and so
to the ambulance that roars down my street
apologies, and to the wretch in the back
apologies too: you come from a place
where pulp's not fiction, you know a world
where bullets are more than metaphors
for lovely eyes, and though I roped you
into my story I'll let you go now, wish you
safe passage through a lifetime of green lights.

Matthew Zapruder

Born in Washington, DC in 1967, he is the author of three collections of poetry, most recently *Come On All You Ghosts*. His poems, essays, and translations have appeared in many publications, including *Open City*, *Bomb*, *Slate*, *American Poetry Review*, *Poetry*, *Tin House*, *Harvard Review*, *The Paris Review*, *The New Republic*, *The Boston Review*, *The New Yorker*, *McSweeney's*, *The Believer*, *Real Simple*, and *The Los Angeles Times*. He has received a William Carlos Williams Award, a May Sarton Award from the Academy of American Arts and Sciences, and a Lannan Literary Fellowship. Currently, he works as an editor for Wave Books, and teaches as a member of the core faculty St. Mary's College of California MFA in Creative Writing. A 2011 Guggenheim Fellow, he lives in Oakland.

Aglow

Hello everyone, hello you. Here we are under this sky.
Where were you Tuesday? I was at the El Rancho Motel
in Gallup. Someone in one of the nameless rooms
was dying, slowly the ambulance came, just another step
towards the end. An older couple asked me
to capture them with a camera, gladly I rose and did
and then back to my chair. I thought of Paul Celan,
one of those poets everything happened to
strangely as it happens to everyone. In German
he wrote he rose three pain inches above the floor,
I don't understand but I understand. Did writing
in German make him a little part of whoever
set in motion the chain of people talking who pushed
his parents under the blue grasses of the Ukraine?
No. My name is Ukrainian and Ukranians killed everyone

but six people with my name. Do you understand
me now? It hurts to be part of the chain and feel rusty
and also a tiny squeak now part of what makes
everything go. People talk a lot, the more they do
the less I remember in one of my rooms someone
is always dying. It doesn't spoil my time is what
spoils my time. No one can know what they've missed,
least of all my father who was building a beautiful boat
from a catalog and might still be. Sometimes I feel him
pushing a little bit on my lower back with a palm
made of ghost orchids and literal wind. Today
I'm holding onto holding onto what Neko Case called
that teenage feeling. She means one thing, I mean another,
I mean to say that just like when I was thirteen
it has been a hidden pleasure but mostly an awful pain
talking to you with a voice that pretends to be shy
and actually is, always in search of the question
that might make you ask me one in return.

Pocket

I like the word pocket. It sounds a little safely
dangerous. Like knowing you once
bought a headlamp in case the lights go out
in a catastrophe. You will put it on your head
and your hands will still be free. Or
standing in a forest and staring at a picture
in a plant book while eating scary looking wild flowers.
Saying pocket makes me feel potentially
but not yet busy. I am getting ready to have
important thoughts. I am thinking about my pocket.
Which has its own particular geology.
Maybe you know what I mean. I mean
I basically know what's in there and can even
list the items but also there are other bits
and pieces made of stuff that might not

even have a name. Only a scientist could figure
it out. And why would a scientist do that?
He or she should be curing brain diseases
or making sure that asteroid doesn't hit us.
Look out scientists! Today the unemployment rate
is 9.4%. I have no idea what that means. I tried
to think about it harder for a while. Then
tried standing in an actual stance of mystery
and not knowing towards the world.
Which is my job. As is staring at the back yard
and for one second believing I am actually
rising away from myself. Which is maybe
what I have in common right now with you.
And now I am placing my hand on this
very dusty table. And brushing away
the dust. And now I am looking away
and thinking for the last time about my pocket.
But this time I am thinking about its darkness.
Like the bottom of the sea. But without
the blind florescent creatures floating
in a circle around the black box which along
with tremendous thunder and huge shards
of metal from the airplane sank down and settled
here where it rests, cheerfully beeping.

Tonight You'll Be Able

It may feel good to go wherever.
Desires lead you into old familiar
destructive awareness. Going a thousand
miles away seems to be keeping up.
Unsettled and anxious signals:
they're so microscope. Be a sleuth.
Tiny sparkling under those around you
sees you feeling and waiting. Life
today is slow moving co-workers.
Respond by giving your profile
a new sense of clarity, and feel
ready to share your outlook even
if they may not be as excited. It
makes you good to spread your joy.
People, it's harder to be yourself.
A series of role playing opportunities
appeases, showing the authentic
you won't hurt anything. Focus
on your lovely find that there
are many more things. Tonight,
you'll be able to talk to anyone
about anything, make all the loved ones
muster up, chat with character,
keep alive the conversations.
You feel you're getting something
someone gives you. The key
to a series of coincidences you
play matchmaker to. An odd couple,
the present you and the future
in a big suit, a new haircut,
or better than anticipated, funds.
A few minor changes to June.
Love partners, your lucky numbers
are 4, 7, 18, 21 and 32. Ask yourself
what would I do if I knew I could
not fail.

Rachel Zucker

Born in New York City in 1971, she is the author of four books of poetry, most recently *Museum of Accidents*. With Arielle Greenberg, she edited two anthologies and co-wrote *Home/Birth: a poemic*, a book of creative nonfiction about birth, feminism, and friendship. She lives with her husband and their three sons, and she teaches poetry at the New York University. She is a certified labor doula.

Alluvial

They say God's voice in the city
sounds like a man but in the desert
sounds like a woman. His voice, the spine
of nighttime, sounds like water.
Rock grazed by streamlets long enough
will sunder. One word against my sternum and

I unzip.

Further Reflections: Commentary on Jewish American Poetry

Myra Sklarew

She is the author of three chapbooks and six collections of poetry, including *Lithuania: New & Selected Poems*, and *The Witness Trees*; short fiction, *Like a Field Riddled by Ants*; and essays, *Over the Rooftops of Time*. A research study on trauma and memory, *Holocaust and the Construction of Memory*, and *The Journey of Child Development: The Selected Papers of Joseph Noshpitz*, co-edited with Bruce Sklarew, are forthcoming. Essays on science and medicine have appeared in *Nature Medicine, Ars Medica*, and other publications. Awards include the PEN Syndicated Fiction Award and the National Jewish Book Council Award in Poetry.

In thinking about this collection of poetry, *The New Promised Land: An Anthology of Contemporary Jewish American Poets*, written by those born after World War II, it is interesting to look back at the history of poetry written by those in the late 19th and 20th centuries. And to consider the makeup of the Jewish American population today. Approximately 15 percent of American Jews today were born outside of the U.S., largely in the Ukraine and Russia, and a small percentage in Israel and Germany. And I would imagine that there are those in small numbers from a great variety of cultures and languages, for example, Ethiopia, Morocco, Iraq. In New York City alone, over 200 different languages are spoken. It was remarkable to hear in Washington, DC, not long ago, a poet reading in her native language, Aramaic, the daily language spoken during the Second

Temple Period, from 539 B.C.E. to 70 C.E., and used in an area of Syria to this day.

As with writers of the late 19th century, like Morris Winshevsky, many Jewish poets represented the Haskalah, Jewish enlightenment, and were in revolt against religion. But what is notable is the extreme diversity, beginning with Penina Moise, born in 1797, who published the first book of poetry, *Fancy's Sketch Book*, by an American Jew, and wrote 180 hymns for use in Hebrew congregations. Other early Jewish American poets include Rebekah Hyneman, Minna Kleeberg, and Emma Lazarus. And writers as diverse as Mani Leib, born in 1883, H. Leivick in 1888, Jacob Glatstein, and Anna Margolin. There were the "sweatshop poets," those who wrote in Yiddish, those influenced by places of birth in Europe, those born in America. There was the group known as "Di Yunge," and later the "Introspectivists," more oriented to the internal life.

Though we make categories, more for our own sake, it seems to me that this excellent group of poets included in this new collection takes us across an enormous spectrum, some who do not address Jewish heritage at all, and others who traverse and make reference to the long history of Jewish writing, from Torah to commentary to Medieval Hebrew poetry, to the lessons of Celan, Zukofsky, and the Modernists. It is fascinating to see just how our younger poets make their way through language and history, their own heritage, a digital world that has changed all of us in how we communicate, and has condensed history in ways that are new. Let us learn from them.

Rachel Barenblat

Rachel Barenblat's biography can be found on page 7.

What makes something a recognizably Jewish American poem?

Authorship? Subject matter? Intended audience? Use of Biblical or Talmudic or kabalistic language and metaphors? Does a Jewish American poem have to be focused inward, or can it also be oriented outward toward the broad world? If a poem operates within the dialectic of nationhood and universalism, tradition and assimilation, is that enough? Who gets to define what's a Jewish American poem—American by whose lights, Jewish by whose definition? There's something about a good Jewish American poem which reaches us in a place beyond language. Like the Abulafian mystics who ascended the ladder of letter-combinations to reach union with God in a place beyond words, we travel the rungs of these lines to that weird, ironic, ineffable, tragicomic, beautiful space where all of our poems intertwine.

Philip Terman

Philip Terman's biography can be found on page 274.

It's a mystery as to why we're drawn to certain sources and not to others, what magnetic forces pull our poetic attention. Judaism provides a good deal of the structures and tropes with which my personality is constituted and to which I'm drawn when I sit down to write. My childhood was guided by two calendars, my poetic education by two traditions. Every good poem transcends any one category. But because I was imbued with that Jewish inheritance, that passion with which Jewish tradition approaches the written and spoken word and the richness of interpretation, I draw from the wealth of images, allusions, figures, and forms inspired by a Jewish civilization which I have always understood, along with Muriel Rukeyser, to be an enormous gift.

Richard Chess

Richard Chess's biography can be found on page 30.

A poem can't declare "Hear O Israel, Adonai is our El, Adonai is One" out of conviction or habit. Nor can it make such a declaration as a statement of its intention. A poem doesn't even have an ear to hear others say what it does not, either out of indifference or because that isn't its truth. A poem can't unify its heart so that it may transmit its belief, when it's lying down and rising up, standing or walking by the way, to its children. No, a poem cannot say or refuse to say the *Shema*, a defining Jewish prayer. So, a poem cannot be Jewish. Not even a poem written in Hebrew, Yiddish, or Ladino. Certainly not in English.

Neither can a poem do *teshuvah*: redirect its life, when it has strayed, toward acts of justice and righteousness. But a poem turns and returns, from the turning of phrases to the returning of consonant and vowel sounds to returning from the end of one row to the beginning of the next. From its first line to its last, a poem turns and returns, with its last line, not infrequently, turning to look back to its first, back to its origins, the place from which it came. Does that make a poem, any poem, every poem Jewish? No.

But in the last few decades American-Jewish *poets* have been turning or returning to the language of Jewish life—religious, cultural, political, historical—as the material of which some of their poems are sewn. A phrase from a prayer here, in a poem that tests and resists or honors and submits to the prayer to which it is now joined. A dream of a poem from there—medieval Spain, Arabic borne by a Hebrew poem—brought over to here—America, English informed by Hebrew informed by Arabic. Languages of Jewish life. Turned and tuned. For the post-chosen—the choosing ear: a new song.

Nomi Stone

A fable, told me by the Jewish community of Djerba, Tunisia offers us a metaphor. In a mythical time, a strange young girl arrived on a raft made of birch onto their island off the coast of North Africa. According to legend, the community was afraid of this new presence and did not greet her. The girl built a hut on a hill and lived by herself. One day, her hut spontaneously and inexplicably burned down, and the community, still afraid, did not come near. They found her later: her body and the features of her face, completely intact. The fable tells that they named her a saint, "The Ghriba,"—meaning the Stranger— and the village built the Ghriba synagogue around her body.

The strata of meaning the Ghriba here embodies might help us think about a contemporary poetics. In Arabic, the word for "strange" also invokes the wondrous and the uncanny. *Das unheimliche*: unlocating us, while at the same time grazing something we almost know. The Ghriba is cast off, on her own, but thereby acquires a kind of marvelous incandescence. Mobilizing this figure as a jumping-off point, I am seeking a poetics that embraces a deterritorialized, roving form of subjectivity. Perhaps language—alternately lush and barbed, drawing from ancientness yet quivering with the new, and ultimately always strange and always familiar—is the only country to which we can ethically promise ourselves.

M. E. Silverman

Some perceptions of renown Jewish poets are more often exclusive of women's contributions to the genre. A list of "best known" Jewish American poets seem to always include mostly men—from Robert Pinksy to Samuel Menashe, from Stanley Kunitz to Philip Levine, from Anthony Hecht to Howard Nemerov, from Ginsberg to

Delmore Schwartz to Brodsky. Overlooked from these lists are some of the best known and widely-cited Jewish American poets—from Penina Moise to Emma Lazarus, from Gertrude Stein to Adrienne Rich, from Muriel Rukeyser to Grace Paley, from Louise Glück to Marilyn Hacker, from Alicia Ostriker to Linda Pastan, from Myra Sklarew to Marge Piercy. While both of these lists exclude poets from this anthology, even a cursory glance at the table of contents reveals an approximate 60–40 favor of Jewish female poets over male poets. Jewish female poets are reshaping what "Jewish poetry" means. They continue to explore a wide range of subject matter including both female identity and Jewish themes as well as every other imaginable theme in a variety of forms and voices.

Ben Mazer

To my mind the great Jewish American poet of the twentieth century was Delmore Schwartz, who influenced me and many of the writers within this anthology. I can remember first being stopped abruptly by these lines—

> Calmly we walk through this April's day,
> Metropolitan poetry here and there,
> In the park sit pauper and *rentier*,
> The screaming children, the motor-car
> Fugitive about us, running away,
> Between the worker and the millionaire
> Number provides all distances,
> It is Nineteen Thirty-Seven now,
> Many great dears are taken away,
> What will become of you and me
> (This is the school in which we learn ...)
> Besides the photo and the memory?
> (... that time is the fire in which we burn.)

—the sense that here was a genuine poet, of a passion and an ineffable quickness in the words, of an evanescence like a cool mountain breeze.

With the publication of *In Dreams Begin Responsibilities*, Delmore's was the most auspicious debut of any American poet since the gradual ascendancy of Allen Tate in the twenties and early thirties. But he seemed to supersede Tate at the time of his appearance, making Tate's near contemporary Hart Crane his true precursor in the line of American poetry. In manner, Schwartz wrote more like Charles Baudelaire, but showed the influence of modernism in the fineness and significant discontinuity of his phrases, formally, and in a brooding regressive narcissism, emotionally. His masters were Joyce and Freud, and his great imaginary rival T. S. Eliot.

Tearing it up as poet and critic in the pages of *The Kenyon Review*, *Partisan Review*, *Poetry*, et al., Delmore burst on the scene like a sky-rocket. With Crane dead, and Eliot in England, Pound safely installed in Europe, and nothing especially challenging them or Joyce, Delmore filled a long vacuum in the development of American poetry, and in doing so filled a very ripe place that had undoubtedly been both unconsciously and naturally reserved for the particular youthful passions, both intellectual and romantic, of his generation, which also, like Crane, had grown up during the heyday of the silent movies, but which had seen them extinguished just as they were discovering poetry. Slightly preceding his great contemporaries Lowell and Berryman in age, Delmore found his poetic fire earlier than they, and in doing so was the first to make the mark of his restless, disquieted generation. He was of that American poetic generation which became inflamed with an interest in poetry during the Depression, during the era of the early talking pictures, during the ascendancy of Auden, and when modern American criticism was just beginning to get off the ground in the *Hound & Horn* in a series of essays by R. P. Blackmur, which came as a revelation to Schwartz, Lowell, and Berryman alike. Delmore displayed his devotional intensity when he published the one and only issue of his magazine *Mosaic* in the wake of the recent demise of the *Hound & Horn*, publishing works by Blackmur, Williams, and other *Hound & Horn* contributors, as well as two poems by himself.

In Delmore's world Henry James and Dostoevsky clashed with Picasso and Mickey Mouse, Bolsheviks warred with Freud and *Ulysses*, and nothing had a historical right to be untinged by a sense of Harvard philosophy (and indeed Delmore pursued graduate studies in philosophy at Harvard, taught composition at Harvard, found a teaching position for Berryman in the English Department at Harvard, and for a time shared quarters with Robert Lowell in a house on Ellery Street). His generation was breathlessly athletic amorously, imitating the movies for their escapism, in their trepidation over the immensely dangerous and daunting world situation, and a sense of impending doom.

The very figure of the late 1930s politically hip Jewish intellectual poet, in his idioms, he suffered deeply from mania, paranoia, and finally depression. His great masterpiece, *Genesis*, an epic verse novel about the coming-of-age of a Jewish boy in Brooklyn in the twenties and thirties (a loosely disguised version of Delmore himself), was unsuccessful critically and commercially, and remains out of print, unread, and unappreciated. As Delmore once remarked to John Berryman, "No reputation is more than snowfall."

Pia Taavila

The literary creations of modern and contemporary Jewish writers, even when touching upon other than Jewish themes, exemplify the *zeitgeist* of the Diaspora. Whether wrangling with what, exactly, is the nature of G-d; or when tracing the trajectory of survival in the aftermath of our birth as a people, as a nation; or when writing upon every imaginable theme that is human, honest, compelling—a spirit of passion and of perseverance permeates the whole. Intellectual pursuits, excellence in cooking, the celebratory nature of lifecycle events and a host of other endeavors and activities in the Jewish tradition shape the minds behind and the essential hearts of these necessary poems. All that our community has endured at the hands of others reminds us of the fragility of human existence, a reality that invites us to embrace our lives with ardor, with an increasingly urgent tenacity. These poems take us to the core of that tenacity in ways that are brilliant and tender, compassionate and insightful. May it ever be so.

Jason Schneiderman

Judaism has no center. There are central texts, central places, and central people, but mostly I think of Judaism as a long conversation. If you think of Judaism as a conversation, then you'll understand why we never stop talking. I grew up feeling shuttled between a secular and a Jewish world. At public school, I was the only Jew, and by extension, the local expert on Judaism. At Jewish summer camps and Hebrew School, I was the only one who couldn't speak Hebrew, wasn't *Shomer Shabbos*, and only waited an hour after meat before milk. At the time, I felt like this sense of displacement and travel was keeping me from being fully Jewish—now I see never feeling quite at home as the central experience of being Jewish. I often look at the insular *Hassidim* in Brooklyn and wonder what kind of Jews can feel so at home! The poetry I value is a result of Modernism, and while the anti-Semites Pound and Eliot are often given credit for shaping Modern Poetry, the major thinkers of Modernism are three-quarters Jewish: Darwin, Marx, Einstein, Freud. And Darwin, as a Christian, was the only one who hesitated to publish. Poetry, like Judaism, has no center.

Joy Ladin

Since the Golden Age of Andalusian Spain, when rabbis wrote poetry in imitation of and competition with their Muslim peers to show which holy language, Hebrew or Arabic, was more beautiful, Judaism has had relatively little interest in poetry. And though American poets from Anne Bradstreet's seventeenth century through Emily Dickinson's 19th century wrote verse that was both religious and literary, and even non-religious poems were often studded with Biblical allusions and quotations, since the twentieth century most American poets with literary aspirations have largely turned their backs on religious language and subject matter. For nigh on a century, mainstream American poetry has largely been secular.

But behind, beside and even within that secular twentieth century mainstream, American Jewish poets have worked to rekindle the synergy between religious and poetic expression that burns so brightly in the Hebrew psalms and the Golden Age lyrics. Charles Reznikoff, noted mostly as a founding Objectivist, wrote many poems riffing on traditional Jewish religious themes, images, language, and ritual, and his many cohorts and successors continue to show how American poetics and Jewish tradition can speak to and through, and revitalize, one another. Perhaps, one day, we will recognize that we are living, and writing, another golden age.

Glossary

Aliyah to go live permanently in Israel.

Baal Tehsuva (also Baal t'shuvah or Baal teshuva) The return of secular Jews to religious Judaism. Translated, it literally means a master of return or repentance. Today, however, it is more commonly used in reference to a Jew who adopts a life of traditional Judaism, after growing up in a home less committed to traditional Jewish practices.

Baruch Hebrew for "Blessed", and is how many prayers begin with Bless the God or baruch atah Adonai.

Beged Kefet term used to represent the Hebrew consonants that use the diacritical dagesh.

Beruryah is mentioned by name four times in the Babylonian Talmud and is the only woman mentioned in rabbinic literature who could be considered a Torah scholar.

Bimah elevated platform in a synagogue where the person reading from the Torah stands.

Bitter herb this is eaten on Passover to remind the Jewish people of the bitterness of slavery of the Israelites in Egypt.

Borobudur a famous Buddhist temple located in Java, Indonesia.

Brucha also b'rachah, which means blessing.

Cantor in Reform Judaism, cantors serve many roles in the Jewish community. They can lead worship, officiate, teach, run synagogue music programs, and offer pastoral care.

Chai is a word that is prominent in the culture. It consists of the letters *chet* and *yod*. Often, Jews wear a *chai* around the neck as a medallion. In Hebrew, the related word *chaya* means "living thing" or "animal," and is derived from the Hebrew word *chai*, meaning "life." Jews often give gifts and donations in multiples of 18, which is called "giving chai."

Charoset or haroset chopped up apples and nuts in wine eaten at the Passover seder. The resulting thick paste is meant to recall the mud bricks Israelites made when they were slaves in Egypt.

Cheder Yiddish for classroom.
Dagesh this is a diacritic used in the Hebrew alphabet. The mark looks like a dot and is placed inside a Hebrew letter.
De Profundis "out of the depths," from Latin. The first words of Psalm 129, and one of the 15 Gradual Psalms sung by the Jewish pilgrims on their way to Jerusalem.
Eliyaho Ha-Navi Elijah the Prophet, one of the greatest prophets in Jewish history and legend.
Golem from Jewish folklore. An animated anthropomorphic being, created from inanimate matter.
Haggadah a text that outlines the order of the Passover seder.
Halakah aka Halacha a collective body of Jewish laws.
Halvah this is a dense nougat-like dessert that some call "food of the Gods."
Haman main antagonist in Book of Esther. Haman and his wife plot to kill all the Jews in Persia; Queen Esther foils the plan.
Horeb refers to Mount Horeb where God gave the Ten Commandments to Moses. Mount Sinai and Mount Horeb are often considered to be two names for the same place, but some scholars think they are different places.
Kippah or Yarmulke a head covering, usually worn in services as a form of respect, but more conservative and orthodox Jews wear them daily.
Klezmer lively music of Eastern European Jews.
Lilith is a non-biblical figure said to have been Adam's wife before Eve. Characterized as a self-assertive woman, Lilith refused to be subservient to Adam and fled or was driven from Eden. Contemporary feminists have adopted Lilith as a symbol of rebellion and bold self-expression.
Lubavich a movement in Orthodox Judaism.
Mazurka a Polish folk dance.
Mezuzah literal translation is "doorpost." Refers to parchment inscribed with words from the Torah. Placed on the doorpost of Jewish homes.
Midrash collection of interpretations, stories, legends about the Bible.
Mikvah is a ritual bath. In many Chasidic communities, men immerse in a mikvah as spiritual preparation for the morning prayer service.
Minotaur a creature with the head of a bull and the body of a man.
Mishuguners Yiddish for "crazy."

Olim the plural form for those who make aliyah.

Passover a Jewish festival to remember the story of the Exodus in which the ancient Israelites were freed by Moses from Egyptian slavery. It begins on the fifteenth day of Nisan in the Spring. It is one of the most widely observed holidays, second only to the New Year.

Piastre refers to currency.

Rebbe a Yiddish word for "rabbi."

Rosh Hashanah means "head of the year" or the Jewish New Year, first of the High Holy Holidays that ends with Yom Kippur. Occurs in Autumn on the first day of the month of Tishrei. The day is believed to be the anniversary of the creation of Adam and Eve.

Shabbas or Shabbat the Sabbath day, which takes place from sundown on Friday until sundown on Saturday every week.

Shavuot marks the spring harvest and the giving of Torah at Sinai.

Shechinah a blessing for the feminine aspect of God.

Shomer Shabbat or shomer Shabbos is a person who observes the *mitzvot* (commandments) for the Jewish Sabbath, which begins at dusk on every Friday until sunset Saturday. The most observant Jew does not cook, spend money, write, operate electrical devices, or do other prohibited Sabbath acts.

Shtetl town, or little town, from Yiddish.

Shuk Mahane Yehuda Market, often referred to as "The Shuk," is a marketplace in Jerusalem, Israel.

Siddur a jewish prayer book.

Sukkot *(sukkōt or sukkos)* means Feast of Booths or Feast of Tabernacles and is a Fall festival holiday celebrated on the 15th day of the month of Tishrei (variously from late September to late October).

Tallis or Tallit prayer shawl worn over the outer clothes during the morning prayers and worn during all prayers on Yom Kippur, the Day of Atonement. The tallis has special tined fringes like knots in each of the four corners. They are first given to a Jew on their Bar Mitzvah (the ceremony that marks them becoming an adult at age 13 in the eyes of the synagogue).

Talmud the book considered second to the Torah (or Old Testament).

Its two components are the Mishnah, which is the first written compendium of Judaism's Oral Law, and the Gemara, an elucidation of the Mishnah and related writings that expounds broadly on the Tanakh (Hebrew Bible).

Taschlikh or Tashlich means "casting off." A ritual of symbolically casting off sins, usually done on the afternoon of Rosh Hashanah (the Jewish New Year), usually into a body of flowing water.

Tepidarium a bathroom, warmed by a heating system beneath the floor, in the Roman baths.

Tu B'Shevat a minor holiday on the fifgteenth day of Shevat or February, on which trees are planted, marking the revival of nature after winter. One of four "New Years" mentioned in the Mishnah

Tzipporah in the Book of Exodus, she is mentioned as the wife of Moses.

Wadi Musa from Arabic for "Valley of Moses." Located in Jordan.

Yarmulke see "Kippah."

Yeshiva a Jewish school or university that focuses on the study of traditional Jewish texts.

Yiddish this language is a combination of German and Hebrew and was spoken by Jewish Eastern European immigrants to the United States in the late nineteenth and early twentieth centuries.

Yom Kippur the Day of Atonement and the holiest day of the year, usually observed by fasting and praying. It completes the period known as the High Holy Holidays, which begins with Rosh Hashanah.

Permissions credits

We would like to thank all the poets for their kind permission to reproduce their work. Every effort has been made to trace copyright holders and we apologize in advance for any unintentional omission. We would be pleased to insert the appropriate acknowledgement in any subsequent edition.

Abramson, Seth. "Hy-Vee" and "Poem for Battered Man" from *Thievery*. Copyright © 2013 by Seth Abramson. Reprinted with permission of the author.

Ager, Deborah. All rights reserved.

Barenblat, Rachel. "Command" published (as "Tzav Pantoum") in *Frostwriting* and in *70 Faces* (Phoenicia Publishing, 2011.). "Eating the Apple" published in *Waiting to Unfold* (Phoenicia Publishing, 2013.) All rights reserved.

Bass, Ellen. "Asking Directions to Paris" and "If You Knew" appeared in *The Human Line*. Copyright © 2007 by Ellen Bass. Reprinted with the permission of The Permissions Company, Inc., on behalf of Copper Canyon Press, http://www.coppercanyonpress.org

Baumel, Judith. "And Boaz Begat Obed and Obed Begat Jesse and Jesse Begat David" from *The Weight of Numbers*. Copyright © 1988 by Judith Baumel. Reprinted with permission of Wesleyan Press. All rights reserved.

Bellm, Dan. "Practice" and "Psalm" and "The Weight" from *Practice*. Copyright © 2008. Reprinted with permission of Sixteen Rivers Press. All rights reserved.

Bernstein, Charles. "Castor Oil", "Of Time and the Line", and "Rivulets of the Dead Jew" appeared in *All the Whiskey in Heaven: Selected Poems* (New York: Farrar, Straus & Giroux, 2010). Copyright © 1991, 2000, 2006 by Charles Bernstein. Reprinted with the permission of The Permissions Company, Inc., on behalf of the author.

Biespiel, David. "Room" first published in *Poetry*, February 2012. All rights reserved.

Burt, Stephen. "Miami Beach" from *Parallel Play*. Copyright © 2006. Reprinted with permission of Graywolf. All rights reserved.

Carlson, Nancy Naomi. All rights reserved.

Castro, Michael. All rights reserved.

Chertok, Alex. All rights reserved.

Chess, Richard. "The Jewish Angel" and "My People" and "Nothing But Pleasure" from *Tekiah*. Copyright © 1994. Reprinted with permission of University of Tampa Press. All rights reserved.

Coleman, Elizabeth J. All rights reserved.

Cooperman, Robert. "Planting Trees in Israel, 1956" from *The Words We Used*. Copyright © 2009. Reprinted with permission of Main Street Rag. All rights reserved. "The Jewish Kid" from *My Shtetl*. Copyright © 2010. Reprinted with permission of Logan House Press. All rights reserved.

Davis, Carol V. "The Art of the Stitch" is published in *Between Storms*. Copyright © 2012. Reprinted with permission of Truman State University Press. All rights reserved.

Day, Lucille Lang. "Changing Trains" from *Fire in the Garden* (Mother's Hen, 1997). Copyright © 1997 by Lucille Lang Day. It first appeared in *Berkeley Poets' Cooperative*. Reprinted by permission of the author. All rights reserved. "God of the Jellyfish" is from *The*

Curvature of Blue (Cervená Barva, 2009). It first appeared in *The Cloud View Poets* (Arctos Press, 2005). Reprinted with permission of Cervená Barva and the author. All rights reserved.

Desrosiers, Lori. "Grandmother's Hands" appeared in *Three Vanities* (Pudding House Press, 2009) and in *The Philosopher's Daughter* (Salmon Poetry, 2013). All rights reserved.

Dolin, Sharon. "Climbing Mt Sinai" from *Realm of the Possible*. Copyright © 2009 by Sharon Dolin. Reprinted with permission of The Permissions Company, Inc., on behalf of Four Way Books, http://www.fourwaybooks.com/ "Your Only Music: Sonnet/Ghazal Starting with a Line from Keats" originally appeared in *Burn and Dodge* by Sharon Dolin, Copyright © 2008. Reprinted by permission of the University of Pittsburgh Press.

Dubrow, Jehanne. "Fasting" and "Judaic Studies" originally published in *The Hardship Post* (Three Candles Press). Copyright © 2009. Reprinted with permission of the author. All rights reserved.

Enszer, Julie R. All rights reserved.

Finkelstein, Norman. "Prayer" originally published in *Restless Messengers*. Copyright © 1992. Reprinted with permission of University of Georgia Press. All rights reserved. "Allegory of a Song" originally published in *Passing Over*. Copyright © 2007. Reprinted with permission from Marsh Hawk Press. All rights reserved.

Fish, Cheryl J. "Generation X, Crown Heights (1995)" initially appeared in *Response: A Contemporary Jewish Review*. Winter/Spring 1997. No 67:85. All rights reserved.

Friedman, Jeff. All rights reserved.

Fuhrman, Joanna. "Moraine for Bob" reprinted from *Moraine* ©

2008 by Joanna Fuhrman, by permission of Hanging Loose Press. All rights reserved.

Gaines-Friedler, Joy. "How We Love Our Parents" originally published in *Like Vapor*. Copyright © 2008. Reprinted with permission of Mayapple Press. All rights reserved.

Gerstler, Amy "Bitter Angel" originally appeared in *Bitter Angel* (North Point Press), reprinted through Carnegie Mellon University. Copyright © 1998. All rights retained by the author.

Goldberg, Beckian Fritz. "In the Middle of Things, Begin" from *In the Badlands of Desire*. Copyright © 1993 by Beckian Fritz Goldberg. Reprinted with the permission of The Permissions Company, Inc., on behalf of the Cleveland State University Poetry Center, http://www.csuohio.edu/poetrycenter

Goldstein, Ellen. All rights reserved.

Good, Howie. All rights reserved.

Gottlieb, Amy. All rights reserved.

Greenberg, Arielle. "Exodus 1:6-11" and "Gospel" and "Synopsis" originally published in *My Kafka Century*. Copyright © 2005. Reprinted with permission by Action Books. All rights reserved.

Grubin, Eve. "The Buried Rib Cage" and "The Nineteenth Century Novel" originally published in *Morning Prayer*. Copyright © 2006. Reprinted with permission by Sheep Meadow Press. All rights reserved.

Hecht, Jennifer Michael. "Naked" from *The Next Ancient World*, published by Tupelo Press, copyright © 2001 Jennifer Michael Hecht. Used with permission. All rights reserved. "Three Boats, One Afternoon" from *Funny*. Winner of the 2005 Felix Pollak

Prize in Poetry. © 2005 by the Board of Regents of the University of Wisconsin System. Read and reproduced by permission of The University of Wisconsin Press.

Hirsch, Edward. "Yahrzeit Candle" from *LAY BACK THE DARKNESS: POEMS* by Edward Hirsch, copyright © 2003 by Edward Hirsch. Used by permission of Alfred A. Knopf, a division of Random House, Inc. "For the Sleepwalkers" from *FOR THE SLEEPWALKERS* by Edward Hirsch, copyright © 1981 by Edward Hirsch. Used by permission of Alfred A. Knopf, a division of Random House, Inc. "Elegy for the Jewish Villages" from *SPECIAL ORDERS: POEMS* by Edward Hirsch, copyright © 2008 by Edward Hirsch. Used by permission of Alfred A. Knopf, a division of Random House, Inc.

Hirshfield, Jane. "In a Kitchen Where Mushrooms were Washed" © Jane Hirshfield. First appeared in *Ploughshares*, reprinted in *The Best American Poetry 2012* (New York: Scribners, 2012). Used by permission of Jane Hirshfield. All rights reserved.

Jacobstein, Roy. "Safari, Rift Valley" and "La Creation" and "Autumn, Geometric" originally appeared in *Ripe*. Winner of the 2002 Felix Pollak Prize in Poetry. Copyright © 2002 by the Board of Regents of the University of Wisconsin System. Reprinted courtesy of The University of Wisconsin Press. All rights reserved.

Kaminsky, Ilya. "Author's Prayer" and "Dancing in Odessa" from *Dancing in Odessa*, published by Tupelo Press, copyright © 2004 Ilya Kaminsky. Used with permission.

Karetnick, Jen. All rights reserved.

Katz, Joy. "Following the Orthodox Men" and "In the Old Jewish Cemetery, Prague" originally appeared in *Fabulae*. Copyright ©

2002 by Joy Katz. Reprinted with permission of Southern Illinois University Press. All rights reserved.

Kerman, Judith. All rights reserved.

Kimmelman, Burt. "Bar Mitzvah" appeared in *As If Free* (Talisman House, 2009). Copyright © 2009. "Mikvah, Warsaw Ghetto 1941" appeared in *The Way We Live*. Copyright © 2011. Reprinted with permission of Dos Madres Press. All rights reserved.

Lader, Bruce. "Breaks" appeared in *Landscapes of Longing*. Copyright © 2009. Reprinted with permission of Main Street Rag. "Ode to Klezmer Musicians" appeared in *Fugitive Hope*. Copyright © 2013. Reprinted with permission of Cervena Barva. All rights reserved.

Ladin, Joy. "Psalm 1:10" appeared in *Psalms*. Copyright © 2010. Used by permission of Wipf and Stock Publishers. http://www.wipfandstock.com/ All rights reserved.

Lazer, Hank. "Torah" is reprinted from *Portions* (Lavender Ink, 2009, 978-1935084044). Reprinted with the permission of Lavender Ink. All rights reserved.

Lehman, David. "A Little History" first appeared in *Valentine Place* (Scribner, 1996). Copyright © 1996. "God: A Sestina" first appeared in *Yeshiva Boys* (Scribner, 2009). Copyright © 2009. All rights reserved. c/o Writers Representative LLC, New York, NY 10011, http://www/writersreps.com/ Published by permission of the author.

Lesser, Rika. "Arrival" © 2013 by Rika Lesser. "Menorah" from *Questions of Love: New & Selected* (Sheep Meadow Press). Copyright © 2008 by Rika Lesser. Reprinted with permission of Sheep Meadow Press and the author. All rights reserved.

Levin, Lynn. "A Misty Day on Mt Nebo" from *Imaginarium* (Loonfeather Press, 2005). Copyright © 2005 by Lynn E. Levin.

Reprinted by permission of the author. "Eve and Lilith Go to Macy's" from *Miss Plastique* (Ragged Sky Press, 2013). Copyright © 2013 by Lynn E. Levin. Reprinted by permission of the author.

Levine, Jeffrey. "Marzurka" and "The Herbalist" appeared in *Rumor of Cortez*. Copyright © 2005. Reprinted with permission of Red Hen Press. All rights reserved.

Levine, Julia B. "Angels" and "Windstorm on the Marsh" appeared in *Practicing for Heaven*. Copyright © 1998. Reprinted with permission of Anhinga Press. "Eighteen Days of Fog and Rain" appeared in *Ditchtender*. Copyright © 2008. Reprinted with permission of University of Tampa Press. All rights reserved.

Loden, Rachel. "Cape Disappointment" first appeared in VOLT. Copyright © 2011 by Rachel Loden. Used by permission of the poet. "What the Gravedigger Needs" appeared in *Dick of the Dead*. Copyright © 2009 by Rachel Loden. Reprinted with the permission of The Permissions Company, Inc., on behalf of Ahsahta Press, http://ahsahtapress.org

Malis, Rachel. All rights reserved.

Margulius, Sandra Cohen. All rights reserved.

Mayer, Liat. All rights reserved.

Mazer, Ben. "Epilogue" appeared in *Poems* (Pen & Anvil Press, 2010). Copyright © 2010 by Ben Mazer. Reprinted with permission of the author. All rights reserved.

McKee, Colleen. All rights reserved.

Meitner, Erika. "Advice" appeared in *Inventory at the All Night Drugstore*. Copyright © 2010. Reprinted with permission of Anhinga Press. All rights reserved. "Yiddishland" first published in *Indiana Review*, 32(1), 2010. Reprinted with permission of author.

Meriam, Mary. All rights reserved.

Miller, Stephen Paul. "Monotheism" and "There is Only One God and You Are Not It" appeared in *There is Only One God and You Are Not It*. Copyright © 2011. Reprinted with permission of Marsh Hawk Press. All rights reserved.

Mirskin, Jerry. "Rock and Water" appeared in *Picture a Gate Hanging Open and Let that Gate be the Sun*. Copyright © 2002. Reprinted with permission of Mammoth Press. All rights reserved.

Moreno, Yvette Neisser. All rights reserved.

Neustadt, Leslie. All rights reserved.

November, Yeoshua. "How a Place Becomes Holy" appeared in *I Just Hope It's Lethal: Poems of Sadness, Madness & Joy*. Copyright © 2005. Reprinted with permission of author. "Baal Teshuvas at the Mikvah" first appeared in *New Vilna Review*. "A Jewish Poet" first appeared in *Prairie Schooner*. All rights reserved.

Novey, Idra. "Instead of" appeared in *Exit, Civilian* (The University of Georgia Press, 2012). Copyright © 2012 by Idra Novey. Reprinted with permission of University of Georgia Press. All rights reserved.

Olstein, Lisa. "Man Feeding Bear Ear of Corn" appeared in *Radio Crackling, Radio Gone*. Copyright © 2006 by Lisa Olstein. Reprinted with the permission of The Permissions Company, Inc., on behalf of Copper Canyon Press, http://www.coppercanyonpress.org/ "Space Junk" and "This is a Test of the Internal Emergency Broadcast System" appeared in *Little Stranger*. Copyright © 2013 by Lisa Olstein. Reprinted with the permission of The Permissions Company, Inc., on behalf of Copper Canyon Press, http://www.coppercanyonpress.org

Osherow, Jacqueline. "Hearing News from the Temple Mount in Salt Lake City" originally appeared in *The Hoopoe's Crown*.

Copyright © 2005 by Jacqueline Osherow. Reprinted with the permission of The Permissions Company, Inc., on behalf of BOA Editions, Ltd., http://www.boaeditions.org "Yom Kippur Sonnet with a Line from Lamentations" from *Dead Men's Praise*, copyright © 1999 by Jacqueline Osherow. Used by permission of Grove/Atlantic, Inc.

Parker, Alan Michael. "Television Psalm" appeared in *Elephants and Butterflies*. Copyright © 2008 by Alan Michael Parker. Reprinted with the permission of The Permissions Company, Inc., on behalf of BOA Editions, Ltd., http://www.boaeditions.org

Ratzabi, Hila. All rights reserved. "Aubade" was first published in *The Cortland Review*, Issue 47, May 2010.

Raz, Hilda. All rights reserved.

Redel, Victoria. "Survivor" appeared in *Already the World*. Copyright © 1995. Reprinted with permission of Kent State Press. All rights reserved.

Rich, Susan. "Different Places to Pray" and "What to Make of Such Beauty" appeared in *The Alchemist's Kitchen*. Copyright © 2010 by Susan Rich. Reprinted with the permission of The Permissions Company, Inc., on behalf of White Pine Press, http://www.whitepine.org

Roberts, Kim. All rights reserved.

Rosenberg, Liz. "Couple on Hospital Elevator" and "How Quickly, How Early" appeared in *Demon Love*. Copyright © 2008. Reprinted with permission of Mammoth Press. All rights reserved.

Sachs, Carly. All rights reserved.

Sadoff, Ira. "My Mother's Funeral" From GRAZING: POEMS.

Copyright 1998 by Ira Sadoff. Used with permission of the poet and the University of Illinois Press

Schiffman, Richard. All rights reserved.

Schneiderman, Jason. "Probability" appeared in *Striking Surface*. Copyright © 2010. Reprinted with permission of Ashland Poetry Press. All rights reserved.

Schor, Esther. "Alef" appeared in *The Hills of Holland*. Copyright © 2002. Reprinted with permission of Archer Press. All rights reserved.

Schultz, Philip. "Why" from *Failure: Poems* by Philip Schultz. Copyright © 2007 by Philip Schultz. Reprinted with permission of Houghton Mifflin Harcourt Publishing Company. All rights reserved. "The Children's Memorial at Yad Vashern" and "I Remember" from *The Holy Worm of Praise* by Philip Schultz. Copyright © 2002 by Philip Schultz. Reprinted with permission of Houghton Mifflin Harcourt Publishing Company. All rights reserved.

Schwartz, Howard. "Breathing in the Dark" and "In that Country" and "Signs of a Lost Tribe" appeared in *Breathing in the Dark*. Copyright © 2008. Reprinted with permission of Mayapple Press. All rights reserved.

Schwartz, Ruth L. "Music for Guitar and Stone" appeared in *Dear Good Naked Morning*. Copyright © 2005 by Ruth L. Schwartz. Reprinted with the permission of The Permissions Company, Inc., on behalf of Autumn House Press, http://www.autumnhouse.org

Serchuk, Peter. All rights reserved.

Seyburn, Patty. "Beruryah, Deciding" appeared in *Diaspordic*. Copyright © 1998. Reprinted with permission of Helicon Nine Editions.

Shapiro, Alan. "How" from *Old War: Poems* by Alan Shapiro. Copyright © 2008 by Alan Shapiro. Reprinted with permission of Houghton Mifflin Harcourt Publishing Company. All Rights Reserved. "Lethe" appeared in *Mixed Company*. Copyright © 1996. Reprinted with permission of University of Chicago Press. "Mezzuzh" appeared in *The Courtesy*. Copyright © 1983. Reprinted with permission of University of Chicago Press. All rights reserved.

Sherbondy, Maureen A. "Tashlich" first appeared *European Judaism* and *Poetica*. It appeared in *Praying at Coffee Shops*. Copyright © 2008. Reprinted with permission of Main Street Rag. All rights reserved.

Shevin, David. "Tiger Lilies" appeared in *Three Miles from Lucky*. Reprinted with permission of Bottom Dog Press. Copyright © 2002. All rights reserved.

Shinder, Jason. "At Sunset" and "Alone on the 5th Day" appeared in *Stupid Hope*. Copyright © 2009 by the Estate of Jason Shinder. Reprinted with the permission of The Permissions Company, Inc., on behalf of Graywolf Press, http://www.graywolfpress.org

Shore, Jane. "A Yes or No Answer" and "Last Words" from *That Said: New and Selected Poems* by Jane Shore. Copyright © 2012 by Jane Shore. Reprinted by permission of Houghton Mifflin Harcourt Publishing Company. All rights reserved.

Siegel, Joan I. "Hyacinth for the Soul" was first published in *Commonweal Magazine*. It also appeared in *Hyacinth for the Soul*. Copyright © 2009. Reprinted with permission from Deerbrook Editions. All rights reserved.

Silverman, M. E. "Bubbie's Kitchen Secret", "The Last Jew" and "Ritual for Learning a History" all appeared in *The Breath before Birds Fly* (ELJ Press). Copyright © 2013 by M. E. Silverman. Used with permission. All rights reserved.

Sirowitz, Hal. "Who Are We Fooling?" appeared in *6S, Volume 3*. Copyright © 2000. Reprinted with permission of author. All rights reserved.

Skillman, Judith. "Let the Cold Come" appeared in *The White Cypress* (Cervéna Barva Press, 2011). Copyright © 2011 by Judith Skillman. "The Theory of Space Travel" appeared in *Worship of the Visible Spectrum* (Breitenbush Books, 1988). Copyright © 1988 by Judith Skillman. Reprinted with permission of the author. All rights reserved.

Skloot, Floyd. "Fiddler's trance" and "Starry Night" and "Yeshiva in the Pale, Jan 1892" appeared in *Selected Poems: 1970-2005* (Tulepo Press). Copyright © 2007 by Floyd Skloot. Used with permission. All rights reserved.

Slonimsky, Lee "Burial of the Sun" appeared in *Pythagoras in Love*. Copyright 2007 by Lee Slonimsky. Reprinted with permission of Orchises Press. All rights reserved. "The Menorah Tree" appeared in *Logician of the Wind*. Copyright 2012 by Lee Slonimsky. Reprinted with permission of Orchises Press. All rights reserved.

Sol, Adam. "Newark, Local" from *Jeremiah, Ohio*. Copyright © 2008 Adam Sol. Reprinted with permission from House of Anansi Press, Toronto.

Solomon, Onna. All rights reserved.

Stein, Melissa. "Olives, Bread, Honey, and Salt", "Want Me" and "Halo" appeared in *Rough Honey* (*American Poetry Review*, 2010). "Olives, Bread, Honey, and Salt" first appeared in *New England Review*; "Rough Honey" was published by the *American Poetry Review*, Copyright © 2010 by Melissa Stein; "Want Me" first appeared in *32 Poems*. Reprinted by permission.

Stone, Nomi. "Outside of Time" and "The Fall of the First Temple, 586 B.C., Jerusalem" appeared in *Stranger's Notebook*. Copyright © 2008 by Nomi (Naomi) Stone. Published 2008 by TriQuarterly Books/Northwestern University Press. All rights reserved. Reprinted with permission of Northwestern University Press.

Stonestreet, Lisa Gluskin. "De Profundis" and "Jars" appeared in *Tulips, Water, Ash*. Copyright © University Press of New England, Lebanon, NH. Reprinted with permission pages 1 and 5. All rights reserved.

Sulak, Marcela. "Pomelo" originally appeared in *Immigrant*, published by Black Lawrence Press. Copyright © 2010. Reprinted with permission. All rights reserved.

Taavila, Pia. All rights reserved. "Lost" first appeared in *32 Poems Magazine*. "Yom Kippur" first appeared in *The Potomac Review*.

Terman, Philip. "The Raccoon" appeared in *Rabbis of the Air*. Copyright © 2007 by Philip Terman. Reprinted with the permission of The Permissions Company, Inc., on behalf of Autumn House Press, http://www.autumnhouse.org/ "The Shank Bone" appeared in *Torah Garden*. Copyright © 2011 by Philip Terman. Reprinted with the permission of The Permissions Company, Inc., on behalf of Autumn House Press, http://www.autumnhouse.org/ "That Lightness" and "The Famous Jewish Russian-Woman Poet Termansky" appeared in *Book of the Unbroken Days* (Mammoth Books, 2004). Reprinted with permission of Mammoth Books.

Topal, Carine. All rights reserved.

Trousdale, Rachel. All rights reserved.

Warn, Emily. "The Rabbi Stumbles" and "While the Secretaries Compose the Engineers' Torah" appeared in *The Novice Insomniac*.

Copyright © 1995 by Emily Warn. Reprinted with the permission of The Permissions Company, Inc., on behalf of Copper Canyon Press, http://www.coppercanyonpress.org

Weiner, Joshua. "Psalm" appeared in *The World's Room*. Copyright © 2001. Reprinted with permission of University of Chicago Press. All rights reserved.

Weinfield, Henry. "Hebrew Melodies" appeared in *Without Melodies: New and Selected Poems and Translations*. Copyright © 2008. Reprinted with permission of Dos Madres Press. All rights reserved.

Weiser, Karen. "A Person Sits Next to a Fugue" appeared in *To Light Out*. Copyright © 2010. Reprinted with permission of Ugly Duckling Press and the author. All rights reserved.

Wetzsteon, Rachel. "Apologies to an Ambulance" and "Six Leagues Under" from *Sakura Park* by Rachel Wetzsteon. Copyright © 2006 by Rachel Wetzsteon. Reprinted by permission of Persea Books, Inc., New York. All rights reserved. "May Poles" from *Silver Roses* by Rachel Wetzsteon. Copyright © 2012 by Rachel Wetzsteon. Reprinted with permission of Persea Books, Inc., New York. All rights reserved..

Zapruder, Matthew. "Pocket" and "Aglow" appeared in *Come on All You Ghosts*. Copyright © 2010 by Matthew Zapruder. Reprinted with the permission of The Permissions Company, Inc., on behalf of Copper Canyon press, http://www.coppercanyonpress.org/ "Tonight You'll Be Able" appeared in *The Pajamaist* by Matthew Zapruder. Reprinted with the permission of The Permissions Company, Inc., on behalf of Copper Canyon Press, http://www.coppercanyonpress.org

Zucker, Rachel. "Alluvial" from *The Bad Wife Handbook*. Copyright © 2007 by Rachel Zucker. Reprinted by permission of Wesleyan University Press. All rights reserved.

www.ingramcontent.com/pod-product-compliance
Lightning Source LLC
Chambersburg PA
CBHW052145300426
44115CB00011B/1524